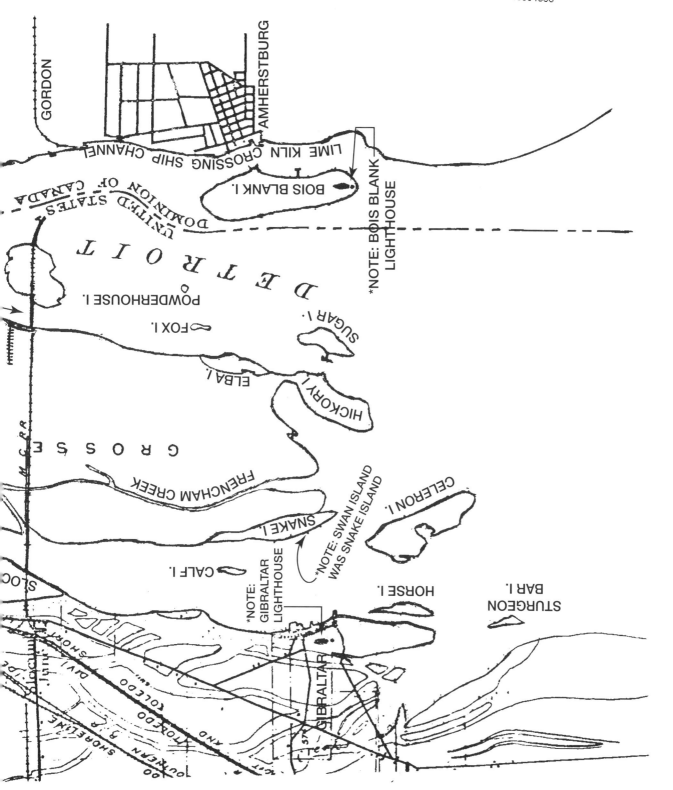

Our "Downriver" River

by Rockne P. Smith

OUR "DOWNRIVER" RIVER:
NAUTICAL HISTORY AND TALES OF
THE LOWER DETROIT RIVER
Copyright © September 1997

by Rockne P. Smith

ISBN 0-9660349-0-2   90000
     4 5 6 7 8 9 10

FOREWARD

This publication is dedicated to all the people who have ever lived around, visited, boated on, or just wondered about the history and heritage along the lower portion of the Detroit River. The "Downriver" area of Detroit commonly refers to all communities that are located along the river from Detroit "down" to Lake Erie. This publication is confined primarily to the nautical history of the communities located on the lower half of the river, the many Downriver islands, and the river itself. It begins in Wyandotte and continues down to the beginning of Lake Erie, including Trenton, Gibraltar, Grosse Ile, Amherstburg, Ontario, and all of the smaller islands.

For those who have boated Downriver, been passengers on friends' boats, ridden the Boblo boats, or have just driven or walked along the river, have you ever wondered what things used to be like before the river became one of the busiest waterways in the world? Who were some of the first people to travel the river? How did they get around? Where were their ships built? When were various area bridges built? Which canals are natural and which were man-made, and when? Who owns the many Downriver islands, and what happened to all the buildings that once stood on them? When were area lighthouses built, and some lost? What really went on during the rumrunning days? Are there really houses with secret tunnels? When were the various marinas, boat launches, and yacht clubs built? Are there any shipwrecks still visible? Was there really another island amusement park before Boblo Island? Is Crystal Bay natural or man-made? And on and on.

As a frequent boater in the Downriver area, it seemed like the more things I experienced along the river, the more curious I became. Then, one of my neighbors gave me a copy of *Gibraltar-Our History,* which is a book on the history of Gibraltar from 1776 to 1976. It is a great book about area history, and it includes some river and nautical history. It satisfied some of my curiosity about the river. Another neighbor loaned me a similar book on Trenton history. It was also a very good book on area history, and it included even more nautical information. This was followed by a Wyandotte book, and others. Each book helped answer many questions about the river for their area, but I could not find any single book or document that dealt just with river and/or nautical history. As interesting as this topic is, it seemed a shame that there was not one single book that a person could read that would cover all these subjects.

This must have been about the time the idea of writing such a book came to mind. Confiding such a plan to a few friends resulted in encouragement and suggestions of knowledgeable people to talk to that may be able to add to the local folklore and history.

After many months of searching local libraries and historical societies, and interviewing many locals, this is my attempt to present *Our "Downriver" River: Nautical History And Tales Of The Lower Detroit River.* Hope you find it as intriguing to read as I did to write!

COVER PICTURES

Leo Kuschel, the renowned Downriver artist, was gracious enough to allow me to use several of his prints as cover pictures and for reference in the book. The front cover has his drawings of the Boblo boat *Columbia* and of the Grosse Ile Lighthouse. Both of these subjects are precious to the Downriver area. The *Columbia* was built in Wyandotte in 1902 and carried passengers back and forth to Boblo Island from that date until 1991. The Grosse Ile Lighthouse was built in 1894 and was in operation until 1948. It is currently owned and maintained by the Grosse Ile Historical Society, which sponsors annual tours of the lighthouse.

A copy of Leo's drawing of the Detroit Lighthouse appears next to a special article he and his wife Sue wrote regarding the Detroit Light beginning on page 129. The Detroit Light is significant to the Downriver area because it is the official beginning of the Detroit River Channel when approaching from Lake Erie. A copy of his painting of the *John T. Hutchinson* is located next to a discussion of Grosse Ile's pay bridge on page 70. This ship is important because it represents a typical Great Lakes freighter, which we are accustomed to seeing on the river system. It is even more significant because it was the freighter that ran into the Grosse Ile Toll Bridge in 1965. For more information on Leo Kuschel's art work, feel free to call his studio at 313-287-6318.

The picture on the back cover is important, at least to me, because it is of my boat! Probably the only historic significance is that it was originally owned by Ricky Hendrix, the well-known NASCAR owner. You will often see this boat on the river and in Crystal Bay. Stop and say hello, and maybe buy a copy of ***Our "Downriver" River.***

INTRODUCTION

The nautical history of the lower Detroit River is presented in four parts:

I. **THE EARLY DAYS**

II. **NAUTICAL HISTORY OF DOWNRIVER COMMUNITIES**

III. **HISTORY OF THE MANY SMALLER DOWNRIVER ISLANDS**

IV. **A GUIDED HISTORICAL BOAT TOUR ON THE RIVER.**

THE EARLY DAYS is a description of the people, area, and happenings in the Downriver area from the 1600s through the early 1800s, including the arrival of the French, Native Americans, British, and early settlers.

NAUTICAL HISTORY OF DOWNRIVER COMMUNITIES includes a separate written discussion of the nautical history of Wyandotte, Trenton, Gibraltar, Grosse Ile, and Amherstburg, Ontario.

HISTORY OF THE MANY SMALLER DOWNRIVER ISLANDS describes the fourteen islands that are located at the southern end of the Detroit River and includes the origination of their names, past and current owners, past and current uses, and other interesting facts and folklore surrounding these many islands.

A GUIDED HISTORICAL BOAT TOUR ON THE RIVER gives you a boat's eye view of the Detroit River starting with Wyandotte, going down the Trenton Channel to Lake Erie, around the many islands, and back to the north end of Grosse Ile via the Amherstburg Channel. Points of historical and/or nautical interest are numbered on a navigation chart to help you follow along and locate each subject.

ACKNOWLEDGMENTS

The information from this book has come from many sources, including books, newspaper articles, personal interviews, scrapbook clippings, etc. The primary reference books include: *The Deep Roots* by Isabella Swan; *Proudly We Record* published by the Rotary Club of Wyandotte, Michigan; *Our Fame & Fortune in Wyandotte* by Edwina M. DeWindt & Joseph C. DeWindt; *Gibraltar - Our Story* by Doris Bobier and Nancy Enyo; *All Our Memories* by Al Roach; *With the Tide* by John Marsh; and *Amherstburg 1796-1996: The New Town on the Garrison Grounds* published by the Amherstburg Bicentennial Book Committee; *Snug Harbor* by Lucy Armstrong Shirmer.

Most newspaper articles, scrapbook clippings, and pictures were found at the Historical Societies of Wyandotte and Grosse Ile and the Bacon Memorial Public Library in Wyandotte. Other information, including pictures and book articles, were found at the Burton Historical Collection in the Detroit Public Library. Other material was graciously provided by individuals from their personal collections.

I wish to give special thanks to the following people who were instrumental in helping me with this project:

Bill Heinrich, a lifelong Downriver resident and mariner, who has spent almost seventy years on and around the Trenton Channel.

Milt Moore, Mike Sieg, and Ron Deneau, Gibraltar neighbors who grew up in the area.

Kathy Marcum, a Downriver newcomer and recent neighbor, who was instrumental in getting the nuts and bolts together to allow this whole thing to get published. Her husband, **Rick,** also helping in many ways.

Jim Engle, who graciously allowed me to photograph many of his historic picture postcards from his prized collection, displayed at his Grosse Ile barber shop.

Good friend **Jack (The Ripper) Dull** who helped with photography.

Karen Risko, a lifelong Downriver (currently Grosse Ile) resident, and educator, who helped with proofreading and other details. She says this project has given her incentive to finish her own book to be published in the near future.

Lynn DiGiacomo, who recently moved to the Detroit area from the East Coast with her husband and one of my coworkers, **Ernie.** She was professionally involved with editing and proofreading on the coast and graciously helped with this book. She is anxious to get involved with other projects in the area.

Michelle Staver, a freelance writer and editor living in Royal Oak. She is an avid scuba diver and enjoys shipwreck diving.

The Grosse Ile Historical Society members, especially **Nancy Karmazin,** who have bent over backwards to help me research their great historical information, including many excellent pictures of our area.

And a special thank you to **Leo Kuschel and his wife Sue,** who were kind enough to allow their artwork to grace the cover of my book, and who contributed a special section on the history of the Detroit Lighthouse. Leo has spent over thirty years studying art, especially boats and lighthouses in the Great Lakes area. He grew up in the Detroit/Port Huron area and had three uncles who served in the United States Lighthouse Service in the Great Lakes. His artwork has hung in the Oval Office of our nation's capital and is currently displayed in every continent of the world.

All of the above spent personal time assisting, and I appreciate their help very much. Others that helped include my boating buddies (especially my year-round boating buddy **Mike Baldwin**), who put up with driving the boat all over the river while I took notes. And, of course, my wife **Coleen**, who let me take all of these boat rides for "professional" reasons.

It was not my intent to research the history itself for the Downriver area. This has been done and recorded very well in the many documents mentioned above. I primarily wanted to pull together just the nautical portion of these total history accounts, which are already in place, and put it in one book. The format for presenting *Our "Downriver" River* will include quotes and paraphrases from the listed references, information learned from interviews with "locals," as well as quotes of newspaper articles written over the years describing various subjects and events.

With the great amount of material and pictures gathered from many sources, I have made an honest effort to include only what appears to be most logical and correct. There have been several cases where written accounts of the same subject and/or event have varied. In these cases, where possible, the differences

were further researched to include the correct version. However, if some errors have crept into this document, I ask for your pardon and kind indulgence. My proofreading and publishing staff have been dedicated and their involvement much appreciated. Hope you enjoy!!!

CONTENTS

I. The Early Days 2

II. Nautical History of Downriver Communities 11

Wyandotte 11

Trenton 30

Gibraltar 49

Grosse Ile 62

Amherstburg 76

III. History of the Many Smaller Downriver Islands 89

Grosse Ile 89

Slocum's Island (Elizabeth Park) 89

Humbug Island 89

Calf Island 90

Swan Island 90

Horse Island 90

Celeron Island 90

Sugar Island 91

Boblo Island (Bois Blanc) 97

Livingstone Channel 104

Powder House Island 109

Fox Island 109

Stony Island 109

Mamajuda Island 110

IV. A Guided Historical Boat Tour on the River 112

Special Article on the Detroit River Light written by
Sue and Leo Kuschel 129

I. THE EARLY DAYS

Very little is known about the Downriver area prior to the sixteenth century. It is believed that a race of aborigines existed in the area before the Native Americans. These prehistoric people, the Mound Builders, were active in Ohio and Southern Michigan. It is known these Mound Builders engaged in industry and trade and acquired certain domestic arts. It is said that what they did, using only fire, water, and rock hammers, would have taken 1,000 men 1,000 years. Why or when these people disappeared is not known. Nor is it known exactly when the Native American tribes, which succeeded them, came into the area.

During the sixteenth century, all of Michigan was a wilderness. The only people living here were Native Americans. The white men came after several men had courage enough to explore the new land. Most of the explorers were men who had been sent by their countries to find a route to China. A Frenchman, Jean Nicolet (1598-1642), is credited with discovering the Great Lakes in 1634. With the opening of this great waterway, people learned that there was land to settle. They began to build homes along the shores of what is now Michigan.

Another famous Frenchman, Robert LaSalle (1643-1687), was interested in establishing a fur trade business from the wilderness of Canada through the Great Lakes to France. He had a ship built in the Niagara Falls area of New York that became the first sailing vessel to move through the Detroit River into the rest of the Great Lakes. The name of this ship was the *Griffon*. Below is an interesting excerpt regarding the *Griffon* from *Our Fame and Fortune in Wyandotte*.

It was a difficult task to build a ship. Winter had come. It was cold and icy. Trees had to be cut from the forest and shaped with hand made tools. The cold temperature froze the sap in the wood and made it hard and brittle. The

Figure 1

The Griffon *was the first sailing vessel to move through the Detroit River into the rest of the Great Lakes. This illustration is from an early drawing based on an old mural.* (Detroit News)

Fig. 1

Fig. 2

mouth of the Detroit River. Here Tonty was taken aboard. When they entered the Detroit River on August 10, Father Hennepin tried to persuade LaSalle to stop and establish a port, but LaSalle did not think it was worthwhile. It is on the north end of Grosse Ile

Figure 2

LaSalle and his men crossing the Detroit River to Canada. (Downriver Michigan)

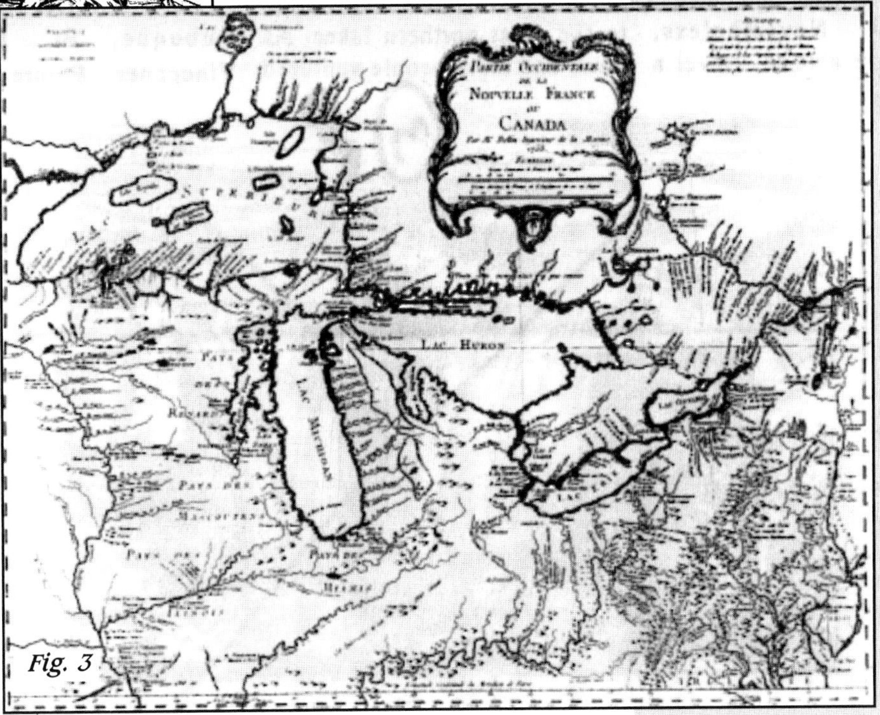

neighboring Indians stole the priceless iron, which had been brought from France to be used in the ships. The Indians were frightened and angry and threatened, because the ship represented extra power for the white men, which meant better business in furs, which they also liked to trade. However, with the arrival of spring, the ship was finished and ready to sail. It was named the Griffon from Governor Frontenac's heraldic insignia. The Indians were astonished and lined the shore to watch the launching of the "great white bird," as they named it.

Fig. 3

On August 7, 1679, the ship headed for Lake Erie and the vast uncharted waters. It was the first ship to sail the Great Lakes. Besides LaSalle, there was on board a crew of thirty-two men and Father Louis Hennepin, chaplain. Lieutenant Tonty had been sent on ahead to the Detroit territory to gather furs in advance.

The story of this trip is told by Father Hennepin in his writings. He describes the first night out as "moonless with fog which forced the crewmen to move slowly with extreme watchfulness." After two days the boat reached the

today that we have a piece of land jutting into the water called Hennepin Point, in memory of Louis Hennepin, who thought that the land was beautiful and good enough to build a fur post.

Two days later, on August 12, this historical vessel reached the lake at the northern end of the Detroit River. Since this was the festival time of St. Claire, Father Hennepin named the lake St. Claire in honor of the saint.

After the Griffon entered Lake Huron, a severe storm struck, and the crew felt

Figure 3

Early map (1770s) of the Great Lakes. (Courtesy of the Bacon Memorial Public Library)

the fury of the lakes for the first time. The boat foundered hopelessly. The crew prayed and made solemn promises of good behavior, if God would save them from the "dirty lake" in the "lost wilderness." The storm did cease and the Griffon *sailed on to St. Ignace and Green Bay. At Green Bay, the ship was loaded with furs for the return trip to New York and Canada. LaSalle, Father Hennepin, and Tonty stayed behind to continue exploring the region and making friends with the Indians. When the men waved good-bye to the crewmen, it was for the last time. The* Griffon *was never seen again.*

No one knows what happened. Some believe the *Griffon* perished during another severe storm on the lakes. Some think her crew turned traitor, sold the cargo, scuttled the ship, went inland, and were killed by the Indians.

The sailing of the *Griffon* on the Great Lakes is important to us because it gave ideas to other men, which made it possible for more and more ships to be built.

After returning to France in 1682, Father Hennepin published several books about explorations and adventures in America. This information may have been available to Antoine de la Mothe Cadillac prior to his exploration of the Great Lakes. Once Cadillac became familiar with the lakes, he advocated building a fort in the Detroit area for checking British incursion and protecting the fur trade for France. He returned to France where his proposal for such a fort was approved.

Cadillac returned to America in 1701 to begin his journey toward the Detroit area. He traveled across Canada by way of small lakes and streams to avoid hostile Indians along the Niagara-Lake Erie route. Indians around that time were scarce in the Detroit area. The region constituted somewhat of a "no man's land," separating enemy tribes.

Once in the area, Cadillac took his party, consisting of over 100 men in twenty-five canoes, south, on what is now called the Detroit River, to select the best site for his settlement. Legend has it that they stayed on Grosse Ile on July 23, 1701, while searching for a good location. Cadillac concluded that the island's wood supply might soon be exhausted by the type of community that he had envisioned. He favored a mainland site at the narrowest spot on the river where no islands obstructed the view of the opposite shore. Thus, they traveled back up the river and selected a spot just below what is now Belle Isle to build their fortress. It is there that Cadillac planted the banner of France, claiming the land of Detroit in the name of the King of France. Therefore, the flag of France became the first flag of Michigan!

Cadillac's plan to establish a fort at Detroit was not well received by the Iroquois Indian Tribe. They held a conference with Dutch and English leaders requesting that these leaders send word to the English King on "how the French encroached upon their territories." They asked the great Father to help prevent such a settlement.

Cadillac was a very ambitious man. He took advantage of all opportunities available in this undeveloped land. He had a vision of his fort becoming an important commercial center with extensive shipping possibilities. He eventually developed enemies, not only among the Indians, but among his own followers as well. As an example of his brashness, in 1707, Cadillac bestowed a land grant to his 15-year-old daughter that included all riverfront land from the Ecorse River toward Lake Erie, including Grosse Ile and the other near-shore islands. These actions, as well as others, caused Cadillac to fall out of favor with French authorities. In 1711, he was removed from the Detroit post and sent to the Louisiana Territory as Governor.

The first people to settle in the Downriver area during the early 1700s were

Fig. 4

Indians known as the Wyandots, also referred to as Hurons. Their main village was in what is now Gibraltar, which was the headquarters for their Council House, Archives, and International Council Fires. They also lived on Bois Blanc Island and in Amherstburg, Ontario. They lived in bark-covered cabins without windows, which were separated from one another by about three or four yards for fear of fire. In many instances, long lodges of bark were constructed to house several families, apartment style. One fire spot in

the center of the lodge served as a community heating and cooking unit. Larger lodges were constructed in the center of the village to serve as a center meeting place for feasting and entertaining visitors. There were few furnishings in the cabins. It was the Indian custom to live out-of-doors as much as possible.

During the middle 1700s, France began to subsidize new settlers who would move in along the Detroit River, with the hope of strengthening their power. Since there was no stone for construction in the area, records show that they found stone on what is now known as Stony Island. They hauled it via large boats, designed for that purpose and powered by oars and sails.

There were many battles and skirmishes between the French and Indians during 1689 and 1763, known as the French and Indian War. These actually became contests primarily between the English and French for control of America. Quebec and Montreal fell to the British in 1759 and 1760, respectively, ending French rule of the Detroit area, and beginning the British era.

During 1760 British Major Robert Rogers, along with 200 men, was sent to negotiate the surrender of Detroit. Journal entries show that their crossing of the Maumee Bay toward Detroit on November 24, 1760, was so foggy that they had to beat a drum to hear each other to keep the boats from scattering. Rogers was met by a band of sixty Indians as they arrived at the west end of Lake Erie on that night. After some bickering, the Indians offered themselves as escorts for the advancement toward

Figure 4

Madame Cadillac being greeted by her husband, Antoine de la Mothe Cadillac, at Detroit in 1701. He built the original fort in what is now Detroit. After falling out of favor, he was sent to become the governor of the Louisiana Territory. (Courtesy of the Burton Historical Collection of the Detroit Public Library)

Detroit. The French surrendered Fort Pontchartrain (in Detroit) to Rogers on November 29, 1760.

Under British control, a new period of development began in the Great Lakes Region. The population grew, trade increased, and ships were built. Among the new ships built were the schooner *Huron* and the sloop *Michigan*, both armed vessels. When Chief Pontiac laid siege to Detroit on May 10, 1763, in an effort to drive out the British, both vessels were anchored beside the settlement at Detroit with their guns protecting the river side of the fort. Chief Pontiac kept lookouts at the mouth of the Detroit River all that summer. On returning from Niagara in June, with men and provisions, the schooner *Huron* was attacked off Turkey Island, thereafter known as Fighting Island. The ship finally made it to Detroit, where it helped break Pontiac's siege in October, 1763.

After the British took over the Detroit area from the French, the Indians still claimed ownership of all the land along the Detroit River, except for a few parcels that they had conveyed to white individuals. These original gifts of land were for "friendly" reasons only. But as time passed, the Indians were induced to part with their land for money and other considerations, not always reflecting honor upon the grantee, and frequently not at all compensatory for the real value of the land.

The British, coming into power, refused to recognize the transfer of property made from the Indians, and tried to keep men from taking these deeds. But the Indians continued to grant properties until the close of the Revolution. Even

after that date, great numbers of transfers went on, some for enormous parcels of land. It was not uncommon for a trader to obtain an Indian deed to twenty thousand or more acres. One deed was for three million acres in the northern part of Ohio, west of Cuyahoga River, and included part of the city of Cleveland. Another deed covered nearly as many acres and included the city of Toledo.

On July 6, 1776, two days after signing the Declaration of Independence, one such deed transferred the title of Grosse Ile from the Potawatomi Indians to Alexander and William Macomb. A deed, or patent, was later signed by President James Monroe in 1812, confirming the real title to the Macombs. The original deed from the Potawatomi Indians is a very interesting document. Excerpts from it include:

Kitche-minishen—Grand Island—or Grosse Ile from the Potawatomi Indians to William and Alexander Macomb.

Know all men by these presents that we, the Chiefs & principle Leaders of the Potawatomi nation of Indians, at Detroit, for ourselves and by & with the advice & consent of the whole of our said Nation, in consideration of good will, love & affection which we and the whole of said nation have & bear unto Alexander Macomb and William Macomb of Detroit, Merchants, and also for divers other good causes & considerations, as the said Chiefs & rest of our nation hereunto moving, have given, granted, enfeoffed & confirmed, and by these presents do give, grant, alien, enfeoff & confirm unto the said Alexander Macomb and William Macomb all the Messuage of Tract of Land known by the name of Grosse Ile & called in our language Kitche-minishen or Grand Island, situate lying & being in the mouth of the Detroit River where it empties itself into Lake Erie approaching the north shore of said river, and bounded by waters of said River.

The Macombs later divided Grosse Ile into farms, leasing them to tenants who built homes and worked the land. Thus Grosse Ile became one of the first white settlements in the lower Downriver area.

For over a decade prior to the acquisition of Grosse Ile, discontentment with British rule had been intensifying in the colonies. The Continental Congress was formed, shots were fired, and the American Revolution began. News that the Declaration of Independence had been signed had not reached the area when the Macombs purchased Grosse Ile. Times were turbulent for the next two decades. Although no battles of the Revolutionary War took place around Detroit, there was much inconvenience and apprehension. The English Crown controlled all transportation on the Great Lakes. Everything had to be carried in the king's vessels, with cargo preference given to the king's stores. Independent merchants were prohibited from carrying their own goods on their own schooners between lake ports. Privately owned craft lay idle. Merchants would neither obtain supplies nor guarantee delivery on contracts. Their stocks became exhausted. Money became scarce, and trade came to a standstill.

The newly formed United States government set up the Northwest Territory, which included all lands that lay north of the Ohio River as far as the Canadian boundaries, and all lands west to the Mississippi River. This Northwest Ordinance was adopted in 1787, and included the Michigan Territory. For homesteaders, the government set a price of two dollars an acre for the land. Many families pulled up stakes and traveled west to establish new homes and fortunes, full of hope for the future.

In spite of the great exodus to the west, the peninsula surrounded by the Great Lakes was bypassed by many settlers. This had nothing to do with poor land, but was the result of being rather inaccessible. There were only two main land routes from the East, the best of which was to come by way of Niagara through Canada, then across the Detroit River, earlier known as "the straits," by crude ferry or any means possible. The second land route followed the southern shore of Lake Erie, where it was a struggle to cross through an area known as the Black Swamp. The third route to the Detroit Downriver area from the East was by water, traveling across Lake Erie by ship from Buffalo, New York. This was risky as often the sailing ships ran into unpredictable storms and high seas on Lake Erie and were wrecked before reaching their destination.

A treaty was signed in 1807 with the Indians, which opened up the southern Michigan territory for settlement. Many Indians still did not want to leave their homes. The Wyandots were a people who were less warlike than many of the tribes and seemed to have adapted easier to the ways of the frontiersmen. They got along especially well with the easygoing French trappers, who had preceded the English and Americans into the region.

The uneasy peace between English and Americans came to a head, breaking out into open warfare in June of 1812, when war was declared against England. It was an especially difficult situation along the river between Michigan and Canada, where close friendships and intermarriages among the French, English, and Americans were common.

The history of the War of 1812 and its impact on the Downriver area has been well studied and documented in many publications; only a few highlights will be included in this edition. Much of the Downriver area was unaware that war with England had been declared on June 18, 1812. One story describes two sailing vessels being sent to Detroit from Sandusky, Ohio, on July 1, 1812. The smaller one was carrying invalids and hospital supplies and traveled along the west course (Trenton Channel), where it made it to Detroit without incident. The larger entered the Detroit River along Amherstburg and was captured by the British in the Bois Blanc Channel.

During the time of the War, there were low marshlands along the whole expanse of the river, and many of the creeks flowing into it were filled with high-growing rushes. This, along with the wooded areas just back from the shoreline and scattered cornfields, gave protection to the soldiers, so that ambush was not uncommon. On August 5, 1812, the great Indian warrior, Tecumseh, joined with the English commander, General Brock, in what is now known as the Battle of Brownstown,

which was a great defeat for the Americans.

Another skirmish, the only one on Michigan soil in which the Americans were successful, was the Battle of Monguagon, which took place on August 9, 1812, only four days after the Brownstown defeat. There are various accounts of this day, but it seems fairly well documented that it took place at Trenton, just above Slocum's Island (current location of Elizabeth Park). The British had taken their position in a heavily wooded area. They included about 400 regular soldiers and Canadian volunteers as well as Tecumseh and 300 warriors. Undoubtedly, the news of the ambush at Brownstown helped inspire the Americans to dislodge the enemy and drive them back. It is said that some of their men were forced from the battlefield onto Slocum's Island, through the deep marshy creek, which then surrounded it. From there they found their boats and recrossed the river to Malden. The Indians scattered throughout the neighboring forests. The total loss of men is not known, but one account estimated the American loss at twenty, with sixty wounded.

Admiral Perry's well-known victory on Lake Erie in September 1813 brought Detroit and the Downriver area under the American flag once more. The treaty that soon followed found the Michigan Territory settling back into a more peaceful routine.

Although the Americans had been victorious, the war had wreaked havoc on all of the countryside along the river all the way down to Maumee. Battles and skirmishes had been fought along the border, and what little progress had been made in the small communities had been nearly destroyed. Orchards, small gardens, and cornfields had been stripped by cannon fire and ravaged by soldiers. Many homes had been destroyed by fire, and the inhabitants had fled for their lives.

Following the War of 1812, the federal government appropriated two million acres of land for the benefit of soldiers. They sent a corps of land surveyors in to examine the land in the Michigan Territory. Their report concluded that not more than one acre out of one hundred, or possibly one out of one thousand, would be fit for cultivation. In spite of such reports, a handful of dedicated men kept their faith in the new territory and doggedly continued to plan for the future. Detroit was the seat of government for the Michigan Territory, and slowly it began to flourish. In September 1818, Governor Lewis Cass met with the Indians still in the Detroit and Downriver area to discuss the matter of getting more land for white settlement. That same month, the Indians signed what is known as the Treaty of St. Mary's, in which they ceded all rights to the reservations still left along the Detroit River. In exchange, they received a tract of some 4,996 acres along the Huron River, which they were to have as long as they and their descendants should live there.

Also in 1818, Governor Cass made his first attempt to establish townships within the Territory. To begin with, he established Huron, Hamtramck, St. Clair, Springwells, and Monguagon. The Territorial Laws describe the territory included within the Township of "Monguagon" as:

Beginning at the southwest border of the said mouth of the River Aux Ecorses (now Ecorse) and running along the shore of the said River Detroit, to the mouth of the River Huron, and including the north shore of the said Huron, and all the lands between the said River Aux Ecorses and Huron.

The chief means of transportation at that time was the river, although there was a crude road, or trail, running parallel with the shore, just a short distance away. Near the present location of Wyandotte was an Indian village called Monquaqu, which undoubtedly gave its name to the Township of Monguagon.

Figure 5 is an early map of the Detroit River showing the location of the twenty-two islands that were scattered along its almost thirty-two-mile length prior to any man-made excavations. Geologists tell us that the Detroit River was formed over 5,000 years ago when the first glacier from the area retreated northward to Canada. The river is 2,503 feet wide at the foot of Woodward Avenue in Detroit, pinching to 1,753 feet where the current Ambassador Bridge is located, and expanding to over three miles as it empties into Lake Erie. During its length, it falls approximately three feet, creating an average current of three miles per hour.

Figure 5

An early map of the Detroit River, showing the twenty-two islands that dot its thirty-two miles from the southern end of Lake St. Clair to the beginning of Lake Erie.

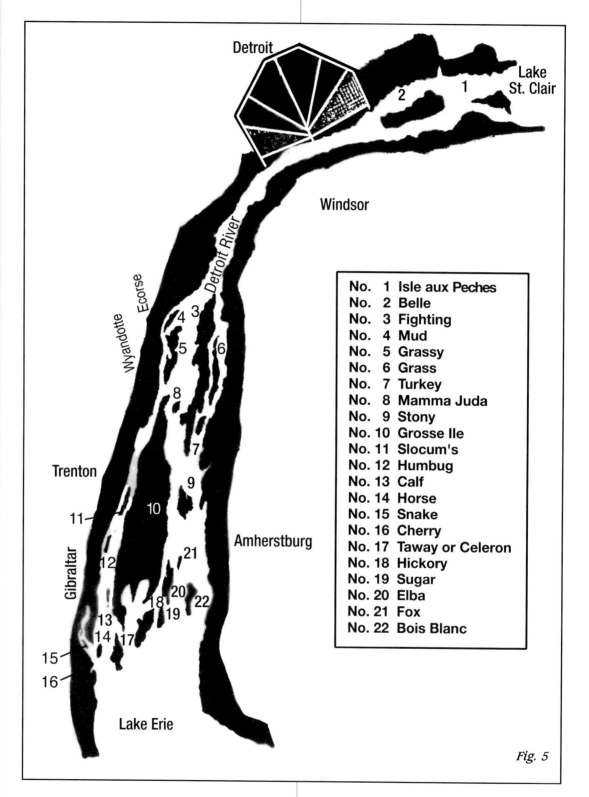

No.	1	Isle aux Peches
No.	2	Belle
No.	3	Fighting
No.	4	Mud
No.	5	Grassy
No.	6	Grass
No.	7	Turkey
No.	8	Mamma Juda
No.	9	Stony
No.	10	Grosse Ile
No.	11	Slocum's
No.	12	Humbug
No.	13	Calf
No.	14	Horse
No.	15	Snake
No.	16	Cherry
No.	17	Taway or Celeron
No.	18	Hickory
No.	19	Sugar
No.	20	Elba
No.	21	Fox
No.	22	Bois Blanc

Fig. 5

II. NAUTICAL HISTORY OF DOWNRIVER COMMUNITIES

WYANDOTTE

Prior to being called Wyandotte, this was an Indian village known as Monguagon, with a number of houses, small orchards, and cornfields. A story of the arrival of George Clark, an early settler into this village, is described in the *Michigan Pioneer Collections*.

In 1818 my father and family moved from Cleveland and Rock River in a boat, coasting along the shore of Lake Erie and Detroit River, up to Monguagon, putting into rivers and bays for harbors at nights and during head winds, waiting there for good weather and fair winds. I came through by land, driving some cattle, assisted by a highly educated young Frenchman, who gave his labor for his board. ... I found my father and family at Monguagon, they having been there several days.

About this time several families lived in the houses, having worked their way up from the States. This was then a noted crossing and landing place for the Indians, their trails branching off into the country.

Game of almost all descriptions was very plentiful in the rivers and marshes. The creeks and swamps teemed with fish, snakes, frogs, etc. Wolves were very numerous; they would give chase to deer, and to escape them the deer would run into the river, and when the river was frozen they would slip down, and thus become an easy prey for the wolves.

George Clark is credited as being one of the first white men in the Wyandotte area. Besides farming, he became absorbed in the fishing industry. In 1833, he obtained possession of Grassy Island, later expanding his interests to include Fighting Island and the area from Belle Isle along the Detroit River to Maumee, Ohio.

For many years, the only sound upon the surging waters along the east boundary line of Wyandotte had been the splashing of the waves against the Indians' birch bark canoes as they plied their way from Wyandotte to Gibraltar and on to Amherstburg. Pioneer George Clark commented on his arrival in this area in 1818 that while on this journey he had noticed only six or eight boats other than the remains of the Perry fleet. The opening of the Erie Canal in 1825 changed this picture and encouraged the influx of settlers from the East.

One of the more famous boats to sail the Great Lakes was named after a Wyandot Indian Chief, Walk-in-the-Water. The ship was built in 1818, near Black Rock, New York, the same area the first Great Lakes sailing ship, the *Niagara,* was built. This boat is best known as the first steamboat to run the Great Lakes. With steam, this ship could move much faster than ships under sail. Her first voyage was made on August 25, 1818. There were twenty-nine fare-paying passengers aboard who paid $24 for tickets from Buffalo to Detroit. It took 44 hours and 10 minutes to reach Detroit. Along the way, she stopped at Erie, Pennsylvania, Cleveland, and Sandusky, Ohio, so people could admire her. She arrived at the mouth of the Detroit

River at night; therefore, the captain decided to lay anchor, so the *Walk-in-the-Water* could arrive in the city during the day for a festive greeting. At Fight-

had not been invented yet, so signals were given by firing a small cannon mounted on the forward deck. The fare charged for first class passengers was $6 from Buffalo to Erie, $12 to Cleveland, and $24 to Detroit. She could accommodate 100 passengers.

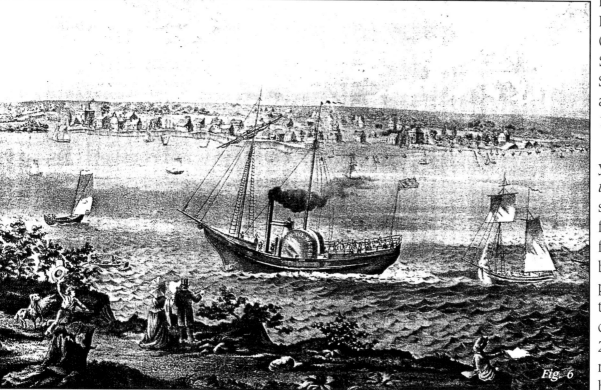

Figure 6

The Walk-in-the-Water *was the first steamship to pass the Downriver shores en route to Detroit from Buffalo in August 1818. It was named after the Wyandot Indian Chief. This painting depicts her on the Detroit River with Detroit in the background. (Courtesy of the Burton Historical Collection of the Detroit Public Library)*

For three years, the *Walk-in-the-Water* sailed back and forth from Buffalo to Detroit, bringing many people to settle the land. Then on November 21, 1821, a terrific storm struck her and drove her ashore at Point Abino, near Buffalo. She was pounded by waves until she broke apart into a total wreck. Her engine was removed and used in other ships for several more years.

ing Island, a group of prominent citizens from Detroit waited to board the ship and ride the rest of the way and enjoy the waiting spectators.

The *Walk-in-the-Water* was a cross between a steamer and a sailing craft, measuring 135 feet in length. She carried two high masts and a square rigged foresail and was said to be "sturdy and fast with an actual speed of 8 mph." A smokestack stood between the masts. Her bow was as high as her stern, similar to her sister sailing ships. On her bow was a carved figurehead of Commodore Oliver Hazard Perry. Passenger quarters were below deck. Cabins were partitioned off for women, men, dining room, smoking room, and baggage. Steam whistles

By 1854, several boats, in fleets or owned singly, were in operation on the river. It was the custom in those days for seafaring captains with a single boat to contract for the carrying of freight. One such schooner, described as "White Sails," approached Wyandotte along the Detroit River. Indians paddled canoes along the river's shoreline watching to see what these white men were delivering in this ship. At the helm was Captain William Bolton, who was the owner and builder of his own boat. He had contracted to carry building supplies for a big project to be built along the Detroit River in what was known as the city of Maquaqua.

Captain Bolton's arrival in Wyandotte was just a beginning of the impact the river would have on Wyandotte. It added cheer, fun, and color to the people's lives, in excursions, boating sport, skating, fishing, etc. It was an important factor in the great industrial picture, allowing boats to bring in raw materials and industrial supplies to the consuming factories. It provided passenger transportation in the days before the streetcar, automobile, and bus. It was easier to travel by water in the pioneer days than land, because the roads were very poor from Detroit and the adjacent areas. It might take a day to travel into Detroit, necessitating an overnight stay. A boat could make it much faster.

Another famous traveler on the Detroit River was the sixteenth president of the United States, Abraham Lincoln. He was attending a Republican political rally in Kalamazoo, Michigan, in 1856. His journey was interrupted when his ship, the *Arrow*, ran aground off Fighting Island. While grounded, it is said that he conceived a method that ships could use to free themselves from such occurrences. It was reported that he actually submitted his idea as an invention and received a patent, although nothing was ever done to promote the idea.

On his first trip of the spring along the Detroit River in 1856, another ship's captain noted that big changes had taken place about halfway between Detroit and Lake Erie. He was referring to smoke billowing from tall chimneys, the fiery glare from red-hot coals, and a roar, from

what turned out to be one of the first blast furnaces in the area. This was the birth of the Eureka Iron Company. It had

Fig. 7

been built on 2,000 acres sold by the Biddle family for $20 per acre. The area was picked for its nearly two miles of riverfront, which provided transportation, and its abundance of tall oaks, elms, and hickories, used for charcoal. The name was changed to Eureka Iron and Steel Company in 1864, when they also began to manufacture steel. In 1865, the factory became nationally famous for running the first Bessemer process in the United States and for manufacturing the first steel rails and iron railroad ties. It furnished employment for the majority of Wyandotte citizens from 1855 to 1890.

After the factory was completed, it was necessary to have laborers. The company advertised in newspapers and with posters in New York City, where boats were arriving from Europe with immigrants seeking a better life. There were no houses for the men to live in when they first arrived to go to work. The original Biddle house was turned into a hotel, and other boarding houses and hotels were built. The first step in city planning began when the officials of the Eureka Iron Company divided the land into lots for houses, stores, schools, and churches.

Figure 7

The original Eureka Iron Company, established in 1856, became the Eureka Iron and Steel Company in 1864, when it also became involved with steel manufacturing. It became famous for running the first Bessemer steel-making process in the United States and for manufacturing the first steel railroad rails. (Courtesy of the Wyandotte Historical Society)

The deed of the village was registered on December 12, 1854, in the Wayne County Register of Deeds as the Village of Wyandotte, named for the John Biddle estate. The original boundary lines extended from Northline to Grove, and from the Detroit River to the present

freight was as important as accommodations for passengers. The loading dock in Wyandotte was located at the foot of Oak Street on the river.

With the beginning of the twentieth century, newer methods of land transportation (namely street railways)

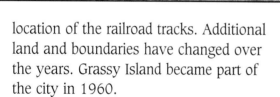

Figure 8

The Tashmoo, built in 1899, was one of the most famous ships built in Wyandotte. It was used to carry passengers to the local islands as well as into the St. Clair River and Put-In-Bay. It eventually sank along the shore at Amherstburg, Ontario, in 1936. (Inland Seas)

Fig. 8

location of the railroad tracks. Additional land and boundaries have changed over the years. Grassy Island became part of the city in 1960.

The height of boat transportation occurred between the years 1880-1889, when pleasure excursions, along with passenger and freight service, were instituted on the Detroit River. Daily boat service followed a scheduled route covering Wyandotte, Trenton, Gibraltar, and adjacent points to Detroit. Some runs included various islands in the river and Amherstburg. Some of these early boats include: the *Jay Cooke*, the *Riverside*, the *Gazelle*, the *Pearl*, the *Massasauga*, the *Evening Star*, the *Wyandotte*, and the *Grace MacMillan*. On all boats, package

Fig. 9

Figure 9

The side-wheel steamer Frank E. Kirby *was built in Wyandotte in 1890, and was a popular Downriver passenger ferry for many years. (Courtesy of the Burton Historical Collection of the Detroit Public Library)*

overshadowed the economic value of the limited package-freight and passenger vessels, which were handicapped by seasonal considerations. In May 1904, the management of the steamer *Wyandotte* found it advantageous to abandon the route. The boat was sold to the Crystal Beach Steamboat Company of New York and used as an excursion craft between Buffalo and Crystal Beach. In 1899, the

Riverside was sold, and it was believed to have continued as an excursion boat out of Cleveland.

The sale of the *Wyandotte* marked the end of extensive passenger service on large vessels operating on a regular schedule. However, Captain DeSana's *Douglas*, a much smaller boat, continued to provide rides between 1904 and 1908, from Trenton to Detroit, whenever passengers so desired. His chief business concerned freight. Passenger accommodations were incidental.

With the closing of extended passenger service in 1908, Wyandotters had to be content with recreational jaunts on the Boblo steamers, the *Ste. Claire* and *Columbia*, or the excursion steamers, the *Frank E. Kirby, Put-In-Bay,* or *Tashmoo*. Or they could rent a boat from Rohmer's Boat Livery located at the foot of Orange Street. In the early 1900s, many families rented boats from a boat livery for excursions across the river, to the islands, or to Detroit, or just for fishing. This rental service was discontinued in 1920-1921, when rumrunning began to dominate the river.

Industrial use of the river has continued since the days of the Eureka Iron and Steel Company. Goods and supplies were brought to and shipped from river docks of local industries during the navigable season April to December. In the days of the Eureka Iron Company, Eber Ward's fleet of twelve steamers, one tug, and three barges, hauled the heavy iron ore and pigs of copper. These accommodations were in addition to the fleet of fourteen steamships owned and operated by his uncle Sam Ward. The names of some of these steamships were appropri-

ate: *Iron Age, Iron Chief, Iron Duke,* and *Iron Cliff.* These were all sold in 1899.

Abundance of lumber provided the opportunity for the construction of several lumber firms and hoop and stave factories just prior to the turn of the cen-

Fig. 10

tury. The chief operation among the group was the D. H. Burrell Company. The factory building, constructed in 1885, occupied the present grounds of the Wyandotte General Hospital. The marshy riverfront made it possible to dredge a bay for a boom, which today is known as a Burrell Slip. Logs were floated down the river from Canada into the company grounds. Wood was also brought in by nearby farmers. D. H. Burrell Company provided employment for 125 people in the making of cheese boxes, hoops, and staves for barrels and kegs. The factory closed in 1902.

The twentieth century chemical-industrial emphasis had its beginning in the decline of the iron and steel enterprise of the late nineteenth century. It was by accident that the economic power of chemicals replaced iron and steel. Through probing of the soil in Wyandotte in search of cheap natural gas fuel for the financially pressed Eureka Iron

Figure 10

The first chemical plant built in Wyandotte in 1891 by the founder J. B. Ford. It was built on sixty-one riverfront acres south of town (location of current par three golf course). This became known as the Michigan Alkali "South Plant" as more buildings were added on the north end of town. The whole complex later became Wyandotte Chemical in 1943, and part of BASF in 1970. (Wyandotte-75 Years of Good Living)

and Steel Company, salt was discovered, which encouraged the founding of a chemical complex.

The first chemical plant was built in 1891 and was named after its founder, J. B. Ford (and Company). It was built on sixty-one riverfront acres south of

on the "north plant," north of town, at the location of the current BASF operation.

The south plant continued to expand until it covered sixty-one acres south of town along the river and both sides of Biddle Street. Early drawings showing

Figure 11

A view of Wyandotte Chemical's South Plant.
(Courtesy of the Wyandotte Historical Society)

mail drop locations at the south plant included these separate buildings: Boiler House, Lime Kilns, Chlorine Liquefaction, Chlorine Cell Room, Carbon Shop, General Repair Shop, Engine

Fig. 11

Figure 12

A view from above the Trenton Channel showing the Wyandotte Chemical South Plant in the foreground, and the North Plant up higher along the River.
(Courtesy of the Wyandotte Historical Society)

town (location of current par three golf course) at a cost of $100,000. Mr. Ford was in the plate glass business, and he started this company primarily for the purpose of producing soda ash, needed for plate glass manufacturing. The business was incorporated in 1895, and became Michigan Alkali. This original chemical complex became known as the "south plant," after construction began in 1895

Fig. 12

Room, Caustic Storage, Chlorine Cell #2, Cement Plant, Cement Shipping, Lye Plant, Yard Mason Shop, Glycol Storage,

Plating Shop, Main Office, Time Office, Scale House, and Dry Ice Plant.

The Dry Ice Plant was one of the last operations added to the south plant. It was built in 1932, as the nation's first dry ice facility, and eventually became

The *Wyandotte*	1908	5000 tonnage	Named for the City of Wyandotte. Discontinued as a freighter in 1962.
The *Alpena*	1909	6000 tonnage	Named for the Alpena quarries.
The *Huron*	1914	8000 tonnage	Named for Lake Huron.
The *Conneaut*	1916	8000 tonnage	Named for Conneaut, Ohio Renamed the Wyandotte in 1963.

the world's largest dry ice manufacturing facility. It operated until 1963, when "the high cost of purifying the CO_2 gas" was cited as the main factor forcing the shutdown decision. The dry ice building was demolished in 1972. Michigan Alkali became Wyandotte Chemical in 1943.

Michigan Alkali bought its own fleet of ships (listed above) beginning in 1908.

The Michigan Alkali fleet was incorporated to facilitate bringing coal and limestone to the company from their holdings in Alpena, Michigan, and Ford Collieries at Curtisville, Pennsylvania. One of the significant features of the fleet was the "self-unloader." The first application of this self-unloading feature on any ship on the Great Lakes was installed on the *Wyandotte*.

As an interesting sidelight, the first captain of the *Wyandotte* visited Wyandotte and the ship in 1958. The following article describing his visit was found in the archives of the Wyandotte Historical Society:

Captain Dudley R. Parsons, first skipper of the steamer Wyandotte *when she was launched 50 years ago, has a spring in his walk and a bright friendly twinkle in his eye after 84 years of work and adventure. Beginning his nautical career as a sailor on his father's sailing schooner in 1893, it was only to be a few years until he captained his first sailing ship (which hauled lumber). It was First Class Piler Parsons when he started on steamers. Soon he graduated to first mate and then to skipper. When the late Emery Ford (father of E. M. Ford, now chairman of the board of Wyandotte Chemicals) prepared to build and man Wyandotte's first vessel, he selected Dudley Parsons as her captain. His starting salary was $1,500 a year, not unusual pay for a ship's master 50 years ago. Captain Parsons had a hand in supervising construction of the steamer, too, as he did later with the* Alpena. *He personally inspected every rivet that held the steel hull together. Whenever he discovered a loose rivet in her, it had to be replaced. Dudley Parsons' ship was to be a safe one, and she was.*

A year later, in 1909, another ship, the Alpena, *was built. Again, young Parsons followed through in supervisory construction duties before taking over as captain. After sailing the* Alpena *two years, Captain Parson's experience in the building of these good-sized lake boats was put to further good use. And, by the time World War I came, he was in charge of the Chicago Shipyard build-*

ing ships to deliver cargoes across the seas. In the early 1920s, he supervised construction of the two I & C Lines cruise ships, the Greater Detroit *and the*

Fig. 13

Greater Buffalo. *These were familiar to thousands of people, for they plied the lake waters as passenger and car ferries until recently.*

World War II came, and he was called by Vice Admiral Emery S. Land to Washington, D.C., and made general inspector of shipyard construction, an appointment that took him to every shipyard under construction in the United States. These yards built the famous "Liberty" ships, that hauled cargoes around the world and played an integral part in the winning of the war.

"She looks a good deal the same as she did when I first took her out in July, 1908." Captain Dudley R. Parsons spoke very much as though he were reminiscing about an old girl friend. And, in a way, he was. Captain Parsons was the first master of the S.S. Wyandotte *when the steamer was launched 50 years ago. The 84-year-old skipper*

enthusiastically toured the good ship Wyandotte *the other day, in the company of its captain, Jack Burdfield, Jim Lucier, Operations Manager of the Wyandotte Transportation Company, and Fleet Engineer Len Thompson. Many new features aboard the steamer delighted the eyes of her first captain. Upon his arrival at Wyandotte, he was escorted through the North Works to the dock where the world's first self-unloading vessel was emptying its hold of raw materials onto the shore. A steady stream of limestone for chemicals manufacturing poured from the raised unloading boom. This was one of the principal reasons for young "Dud" Parsons wanting to skipper the* Wyandotte. *It was something "new and different." Here on the Great Lakes was the first boat to unload itself. Its original unloading boom was 80 feet long. Now the boom is 120 feet long, or 40 feet longer than when the captain first took her into the water. Today's ocean-going ships are beginning to issue their own versions of the unloading boom first incorporated in the design of the* Wyandotte *of '08. Proof enough of the farsighted thinking of those who built the first in our fleet. This boat is still in active service, also, because she has kept up with the times. Fully modern, up-to-date navigational aids constitute the most notable single improvement to the shipshape coal and limestone carrier, in Captain Parsons' opinion. In the pilot house, he found complete ship-to-shore radio-telephone facilities to keep the vessel in constant contact with the shore. Radio direction finder and radar equipment for efficient navigation despite poor visibility which frequently occurs, and a gyro compass that is a far cry from compasses of 50 years ago. A 60 foot addition to the steamer's length was not new to the "skipper," as this was done in 1910 while he was captain of our second boat, the* Alpena. *The dining room continues to serve delicious meals and a cup of coffee (the captain paused for one). A big icebox in the galley has long since been replaced by a modern refrigeration unit in the same size space. There's more room for food now, since there's no further need to stow enough ice for a trip's duration. To shorten a long story, the steamer* Wyandotte *retains enough of the old, and has added enough of the new, to keep her a seaworthy and efficient member of the Wyandotte Chemicals Fleet.*

In addition to the fleet listed on page 17, the Wyandotte Chemicals Corporation occasionally rented two other ships, the *Michigan* and *Blue Line*, which hauled caustic soda liquid to eastern storage points. In 1954, the Wyandotte Transportation Company purchased three boats: The *General Orlando M. Poe*, the *F. B. Morse*, and the *Odanah*. These boats were converted into barges to transport chemicals from the company to Chicago, and then to river barges for a trip down the Mississippi. The complete fleet was liquidated in the 1960s.

After the establishment of the first chemical industry, Wyandotte became the site of a proliferation of chemical operations. The Pennsylvania Salt Company developed a branch at the south end of town in 1900. In 1955, it merged with another company. The name was changed to Penn Salt in 1957. In 1969,

another merger with Wallace Tiernan wrought a change in name again to Pennwalt Corporation. Many other chemical companies, including E.I. DuPont de Nemours, began operations in Wyandotte during the early years of the twentieth century.

One of the more recent significant historical events affecting Wyandotte occurred in 1969, when the Wyandotte Chemicals Corporation placed 100,000

shares of its stock on the open market for the first time. Eventually, 98 percent of the stock was acquired by the German firm of Badische Aniline Soda Fabrik, or better known as BASF Corporation. The Wyandotte Chemical family heirs withdrew their official connection with the firm, and management changed hands to BASF in 1970.

Another important Wyandotte industry directly "affecting" and "being affected by" the Detroit River was shipbuilding. Eber Ward established this significant operation in 1871. The machine shop

Figure 14

Detroit Dock Company located in Wyandotte at the foot of Plum Street. It was started by Eber Ward in 1871. The first iron-hulled ship, the E. B. Ward, was launched in 1872. At least thirty ships were built there

before his death. The American Shipbuilding Company took over in 1899. They primarily built steel hulls, which were then towed to their Detroit Plant, where they were completed.
(Wyandotte-75 Years of Good Living)

and docks were constructed at the south end of town at the foot of Plum Street. The first iron ship built in Wyandotte was the *E. B. Ward*, launched in August 1872. Thirty ships were built before Ward's death. Upon his death the shipyards passed into the hands of the Detroit Dock Company. They continued in operational control of the shipyards until 1899, when the American Shipbuilding Company, a trust composed of several companies including the Detroit Dry Dock, assumed the management until closing the yards in 1922. The Wyandotte plant was essentially for hull construction, while the Detroit plant built the boilers, machinery, and upper works. After launching the hull, it would be towed to Detroit for finishing.

One of the more famous side-wheel passenger ships, the *Frank E. Kirby*, was launched on Lincoln's birthday in 1890. Many stories have been told about her being challenged and accepting races around the river and Lake Erie. She was a success from the start, winning all races. She also set the record for the sixty-mile trip between Detroit and Put-In-Bay at 2 hours and 50 minutes. Every Wyandotter loved the *Kirby*; she symbolized days of laughter, and the joy of excursions, picnics, and other good times. For many years she ran the route to Put-In-Bay. Every church, school, and lodge boarded the *Kirby* for their special outings. The *Put-In-Bay* entered the route in 1911, but the *Kirby* continued to sail until she was sold in 1920. In recognition of her unexcelled speed and efficiency, and the significance and romanticism of her name, her engine

rests today at the Henry Ford Museum. The *Put-In-Bay* was retired and burned in 1953.

The steamer *Wyandotte* was launched on July 16, 1892. It was the pride of every person in Wyandotte, being named in honor of the city. To consummate the launching, the public was invited to board, inspect, and enjoy a free ride. Said to be the fastest and best equipped, the *Wyandotte* also had the most accommodations of any steamboat on the Great Lakes. The smoking room located on the lower deck impressed the male passengers with its interior finish of oak. The ladies swooned over the exquisite carpets, furniture, and tasteful furnishing found everywhere, including the ladies' retiring room. Children were impressed that this beautiful ship could make the trip from Detroit in only thirty-five minutes.

Perhaps the most famous of all ships built in Wyandotte is the *Tashmoo*. It was launched December 30, 1899. At 308 feet in length, a beam of 37 1/2 feet, and draft of 8 feet, she was a large excursion boat. Her overall width, including the paddle wheels, was 69 feet. Her owners, the White Star Line, made history when they were coerced into betting The Cleveland and Buffalo Transportation Company $1,000 that the *Tashmoo* could beat their pride and joy, *City of Erie*, in a straight 94-mile race between Cleveland and Erie, Pennsylvania.

Following are excerpts from *Inland Seas*, a quarterly journal of The Great Lakes Historical Society describing the race:

LAKE ERIE'S FIRST AND LAST GREAT OFFICIAL STEAMER RACE

by Kathy Warren

This event began on the balmy morning of June 4, 1901. Thousands of spectators lined the Cleveland, Ohio, waterfront to watch. The spectators inspected the steamer, "City of Erie," owned by the Cleveland and Buffalo Transportation Company while she was moored in the Cuyahoga River. Passengers hurried ashore. Stevedores unloaded her freight cargo on the deck.

She had just arrived in Cleveland early that morning on her regular run from Buffalo, but her return trip was scheduled to be anything but routine. There were ripples of excitement among the debarking passengers and the people lining the decks and waterfront offices. They were waiting for the race to begin between the "City of Erie" and the steamer "Tashmoo" from Detroit.

The "Tashmoo," nicknamed the "The White Flyer," was the pride of her owners, the White Star Line. Yesterday, the "Tashmoo" had steamed into Cleveland harbor and spent the night behind the breakwater, watched over by her captain, B. S. Baker, well-known Detroit Skipper.

The weather seemed to favor the race. The surface of Lake Erie seemed as smooth as the cloudless blue sky. The breeze whispered gently and did not work itself into one of the famous short-notice Lake Erie gales.

Aboard the "City of Erie," Captain Hugh McAlpine prodded the already busy crew to stow the lifeboats on the lower deck to eliminate wind resistance and for the same reason—take down the flagpoles. Sweating men readied the engines for the race, and chief Engineer Rendall was everywhere at once, trying to insure that nothing would go wrong. Below deck, firemen stoked the coal and discarded all stony-looking pieces that might turn into fire-box clinkers. Every crew member on the "City of Erie" was staking his life, sacred honor and, in many cases, worldly fortunes on the race. They and the Ohioans at the waterfront cheered the "City of Erie" with fervor.

The backers of the "Tashmoo" were just as loud. Detroiters and people from along the St. Clair and Detroit Rivers were in the crowd betting on and cheering on their sleek, river speed queen.

Government inspectors watched to see that no laws were broken. The racing course for the two extended straight along the south shore of Lake Erie, starting from a line off the waterworks crib six miles outside of the Cleveland breakwater and ended at a line ten miles off Presque Isle lighthouse at Erie, Pennsylvania, almost one hundred miles. The nearest point of land was Fairport, Ohio, where the steamers would pass about two and one half miles off shore.

The two steamers worked abreast of each other as they neared the starting line. Each shut off her engines. The little cannon on the tug boat at the starting line boomed, bells clanged aboard the steamers and their paddle wheels churned the water. Harbor boats blew their whistles and factory whistles joined in until the air vibrated.

Figure 15

The City of Erie *which raced the* Tashmoo *from Cleveland to Erie, Pennsylvania, in 1901 is pictured here.* (Inland Seas) *The* City of Erie *ended up winning one of the most famous races of the time. (See page 14 for a picture of* Tashmoo.)

Records show that the "City of Erie" crossed the starting line a few seconds ahead of the "Tashmoo," but slowly the "Tashmoo" caught up. The two steamers ran bow to bow for about an hour. Swells from the wash of the steamers battered the shore and clouds of smoke, steam and spray followed.

The steamers thrashed past Ashtabula Harbor and "City of Erie" pulled abreast of the "Tashmoo." Gradually she forged ahead and when they passed Conneaut, the "City of Erie" was about two lengths ahead. Twenty miles from the finish line,

small sheet of tissue paper, fasten it to the bird's leg and turn it loose. When the pigeon reached home, willing hands took the paper and hurried the message to the newspaper. Some reporters tossed their messages overboard in sealed tin cans. Small boats waiting at predetermined spots along the route grabbed the cans and hurried ashore to the telegraph.

The "City of Erie" maintained her lead from twenty miles short of the finish line until both steamers chugged across it. The officials in the timekeepers' and judges' boats marking the finish line

Fig. 15

the "City of Erie" was three lengths in the lead.

Newspaper reporters aboard the racing steamers assigned to cover the event had to use ingenuity to get their reports ashore and into their city rooms. Some used carrier pigeons. As one ship or the other would change position, the reporters would scribble the news on a

were tossed around in the turbulence as the giant racers beat water, but their top watches weren't stopped from recording the close finish. The Bow of "City of Erie" crossed the finish line just forty-five seconds ahead of "Tashmoo."

This was the last great (official) race between two large steam boats on the Great Lakes. Maritime officials frowned *upon such races for safety reasons and ship owners weren't too anxious to expose their vessels to the strain and expense.*

Both the "Tashmoo" and the "City of Erie" suffered tragic old ages. The "City of Erie" made her last trip for the C & B Line between Buffalo and Cleveland in the fall of 1937. That winter she was moored alongside her sistership, the "City of Buffalo," at the East Ninth Street Pier in Cleveland. In March of 1938, the "City of Buffalo" caught fire and burned. The "City of Erie" escaped the flames, but not the wreckers' tools.

The trim, white "Tashmoo" met a similar fate. Her last voyage was down the Detroit River for an evening cruise on June 18, 1936. She carried about fourteen hundred passengers, most of them dancing and having a good time. In the dark the "Tashmoo" hit what is believed to have been a loose rock in the channel and tore a gaping hole below the water line.

She headed immediately for the nearest dock which was at Amherstburg on the Canadian side. With her orchestra still playing and her passengers still dancing, unaware of their peril, the "Tashmoo" rushed to dock. All of the passengers were safely landed and a major lake disaster was narrowly averted.

The "Tashmoo" sank at the dock soon after stopping in about fifteen feet of water, with her upper decks still well above water. Her owners eventually abandoned her to wreckers. The "Tashmoo" career ended the same as the "City of Erie," but for a brief moment in time, they shared the distinction of setting new speed records in Great

Lakes history.

There have been many articles written about this race. Some give more details regarding how both ships prepared for the race. The *Tashmoo* made some minor equipment changes, while the *City of Erie* actually made several significant changes to enhance performance, such as stowing dry ice to be used later to cool the steam condensers. They also removed unneeded weight and made other streamlining improvements, while the *Tashmoo* was left pretty much the same as when it was used to haul passengers. Once under way, the *Tashmoo* crew realized they were having trouble keeping up, they actually moved two big grand pianos, as well as other furniture, toward the bow while running, trying to get the ship better balanced. There were reports also that a total of over one million dollars had been wagered on the outcome of this single race.

Following this great steamboat race, the *Tashmoo* spent most of her life carrying passengers on the local front between Detroit, Wyandotte, Sugar Island, Amherstburg, Put-In-Bay, Toledo, etc. until her untimely sinking in 1936. Her wheelhouse ended its life on top of a boat house in Grosse Ile.

At the outbreak of World War I, local Wyandotte contracts were received to build Norwegian and English cargo ships. After the United States entered the war, all ships built were built for the United States Merchant Marine. During peacetime, the shipbuilding crew varied from 100 to 700 men. However, employment reached a peak of 4,000 during World War I, requiring ten paymasters to pay the workers each Saturday.

Launching of ships was a festive occasion. Housewives left their housework, schools were dismissed, and the heavy atmosphere of suspense and excitement hung over the city each day a ship was completed. A breathless tension preceded the sound of a crashing champagne bottle each time a boat slid down the ways into the deep blue of the Detroit River.

The building of large ships was discontinued following World War I. In its place, several independent builders took advantage of the location along the river and opened shops that built smaller crafts and pleasure boats. All Wyandotte shipbuilding was discontinued by 1920, in favor of more modern twentieth-century manufacturing.

Over the fifty years that this industry was in operation, between 200 and 300 ships were built and launched in Wyandotte for commercial use on the Great Lakes. Nearly every family in town had a member working at the shipyards during the years of operation. Following is a list of ships built in Wyandotte (list from *Proudly We Record*, compiled from notebooks kept by Bert Conwell and Moses Widner, former employees of shipyard):

E B. Ward 1872
Queen of the Lake 1873
Sport .1873
Grace McMillan 1879
City of Cleveland . . . . . . .June 23, 1880
Car Ferry Transport 1880
Boston 1880
Lehigh 1880
City of Milwaukee . . . . . .Feb 11, 1881
Wisconsin 1882
Michigan 1882
Clarion 1882
Brunswick 1882

City of Mackinac 1883
Car Ferry Michigan Central 1883
Albany 1884
Syracuse 1884
Car Ferry Landsdown . . .May 10, 1885
City Of Cleveland . . . . . . .Sept. 9, 1885
Maskotte . . . . .April 27, 1885
Susan E. Peck . . . . .July 29, 1886
Fayette Brown . . . . .May 14, 1887
E. M. Peck . . . . .May 3, 1888
Hudson . . . . .Nov 16,1888
Harlem . . . . .July 3, 1888
City of Detroit . . . . .Sept 26, 1888
Thomas W. Palmer . . . . . . .Feb 9, 1889
Manchester . . . . .May 4, 1889
Livingstone . . . . .May 18, 1889
John Owen . . . . .June 25, 1889
Stephen R. Kirby . . . . . .May 24, 1890
Frank E. Kirby . . . . .Feb 12, 1890
Maryland . . . . .July 14, 1890
Marigold . . . . .Nov 15, 1890
E. C. Pope . . . . .May 2, 1891
Pioneer . . . . .May 7, 1892
Mahoning . . . . .June 18, 1892
Wyandotte . . . . .July 16, 1892
Selwyn Eddy . . . . .Dec 3, 1892
City of Alpena . . . . .Mar 13, 1893
Mohawk . . . . .May 20, 1893
City of Mackinac . . . . . . .Mar 13, 1893
Harvey H. Brown . . . . . .May 27, 1893
Arrow . . . . .Mar 14, 1894
Argo .1895
City of Buffalo . . . . .Dec 24, 1895
Senator . . . . .June 20, 1896
Aragon . . . . .May 23, 1896
Sir William Fairbairn . . . . .Aug 1, 1896
Robert Fulton . . . . .April 2, 1898
Troy . . . . .July 20, 1898
Pennsylvania 1899
United States Tug
Gen. McWilliams 1899
Tashmoo . . . . .Dec 30, 1899
Angeline . . . . .Sept 3, 1899
Admiral . . . . .Nov 18, 1899

Harvard . . . . .May 19, 1900
Simon J. Murphy . . . . . .June 23, 1900
Howard L. Shaw . . . . . . .Sept 15, 1900
James Battle . . . . .Oct 13, 1900
David C. Whitney . . . . . . .Jan 19, 1901
Mars . . . . .Mar 9, 1901
Uranus . . . . .April 20, 1901
Hugoma . . . . .Oct 5, 1901
Colonel . . . . .July 13, 1901
Yosemite . . . . .Sept 7, 1901
Eastern States . . . . .Dec 7, 1901
Western States . . . . .Jan 18, 1902
Greyhound . . . . .Feb 15, 1902
William Fitch . . . . .April 12, 1902
Columbia (Boblo Boat) . .May 10, 1902
Munsey . . . . .Sept 20, 1902
Tionesta . . . . .Dec 15, 1902
S. N. Parent . . . . .Feb 28, 1903
Albert M. Marshall . . . .June 27, 1903
A. D. Davidson . . . . .Aug 6, 1903
James H. Reid . . . . .May 28, 1903
Western Star . . . . .Oct 3, 1903
F. & P. M. No. 14 . . . . . .Dec 19, 1903
Utica . . . . .April 28, 1904
Amasa Stone . . . . .Mar 15, 1905
Lyman P. Smith . . . . . .May 27, 1905
Powell Stack House . . . . .Aug 5, 1905
W. K. Bixby . . . . .Nov 15, 1905
E. D. Carter . . . . .Jan 13, 1906
Harry Coulby . . . . .Mar 24, 1906
Sir Thomas
Shaughnessy . . . . .May 19, 1906
Samuel Mather . . . . . . .July 28, 1906
Brittania . . . . .May 12, 1906
W. E. Fitzgerald . . . . . .Sept 15, 1906
City of Cleveland . . . . . . .Jan 5, 1907
J. H. Bartow . . . . .Feb 9, 1907
Charles O. Jenkins . . . . .June 29, 1907
Calumet . . . . .Aug 10, 1907
Edwin H. Ohl . . . . . . .Sept 28, 1907
Thomas Barlum . . . . . . .Nov 21, 1907
Wainwright . . . . .Jan 25, 1908
A. E. Nettleton . . . . . . .April 11, 1908
Alpena . . . . .Mar 24, 1909
Benjamin Noble . . . . . . .April 28, 1909

Conemaugh . . . . .June 24, 1909
Rochester . . . . .Sept 4, 1909
Octorara . . . . .Dec 11, 1909
Arlington . . . . .Mar 19, 1910
Brandon . . . . .Mar 19, 1910
E. H. Utley . . . . .May 14, 1910
Allegheny . . . . .July 9, 1910
Put-In-Bay . . . . .Mar 25, 1911
City of Detroit . . . . .Oct 7, 1911
Calcite . . . . .Mar 30, 1912
Lucius W. Robinson . . . .April 20, 1912
Seeandbee . . . . .Nov 9, 1912
A. D. MacTier . . . . .Mar 8, 1913
F. P. Jones . . . . .Mar 8, 1913
Drill Boat No. 1 . . . . . . .April 26, 1913
Adrian Islin . . . . .Mar 11, 1914
George L. Eaton . . . . . .Mar 11, 1916
Gisla . . . . .Mar 11, 1916
Gaute . . . . .May 3, 1916
Vestland . . . . .June 24, 1916
Levisa . . . . .Aug 12, 1916
Lars Fostenes . . . . .Sept 7, 1916
Ozama . . . . .Oct 7, 1916
Carib . . . . .Oct 28, 1916
Bacchus . . . . .Jan 6, 1917
War Patrol . . . . .Jan 29, 1917
Angers . . . . .April 10, 1917
War Major . . . . .April 10, 1917
War Tune . . . . .May 10, 1917
Labor . . . . .June 7, 1917
War Song . . . . .July 25, 1917
War Path . . . . .Aug 11, 1917
War Beaver . . . . .Sept 22, 1917
War Honour . . . . .Oct 10, 1917
War Fox . . . . .Nov 3, 1917
War Martin . . . . .Nov 24, 1917
War Ferret . . . . .Dec 29, 1917
War Hope . . . . .Jan 19, 1918
War Palm . . . . .Feb 16, 1918
War Swift . . . . .Mar 2, 1918
War Thrush . . . . .Mar 20, 1918
War Lynx . . . . .April 20, 1918
Lake Ennis . . . . .April 27, 1918
Lake Largo . . . . .May 11, 1918
Lake Lasang . . . . .May 22, 1918

Figure 16

The "stocks," part of the framework used during shipbuilding days in Wyandotte. (Courtesy of the Bacon Memorial Public Library)

Figure 17

After the "stocks" were removed during shipbuilding in Wyandotte. (Wyandotte - 75 Years of Good Living)

Lake Daraga	June 12, 1918
Lake Damita	June 26, 1918
Lake Benbow	July 4, 1918
Lake Gahona	July 12, 1918
Lake Ormoc	July 25, 1918
Lake Akkra	Aug 10, 1918
Lake Licking	Aug 24, 1918
Lake Ypsilanti	Aug 31, 1918
Goodspeed	Sept 14, 1918
Goree	Sept 19, 1918
Lake Gorin	Sept 26, 1918
Lake Gormania	Sept 30, 1918
Lake Grondon	Oct 23, 1918
Lake Graphite	Oct 29, 1918
Lake Gratis	Nov 6, 1918
Lake Grattan	Nov 27, 1918
Lake Gravella	Dec 7, 1918
Lake Gravett	Nov 13, 1918

Lake Gravity	Dec 24, 1918
Lake Greenbrier	Jan 29, 1919
Lake Gretna	Jan 16, 1919
Lake Grogan	Jan 20, 1919
Lake Flovilla	Jan 20, 1919
Lake Flume	Feb 6, 1919
Lake Flushing	Feb 12, 1919
Lake Flynus	Feb 15, 1919
Lake Folcroft	Feb 27, 1919
Lake Sapor	Feb 27, 1919
Lake Fonda	Mar 13, 1919
Lake Fontana	Mar 27, 1919
Lake Fontanet	Mar 19, 1919
Lake Faresman	April 2, 1919
Lake Gilboa	April 24, 1919
Lake Gilpen	April 29, 1919
Lake Gilta	May 20, 1919
Lake Giltedge	May 12, 1919
Lake Girth	June 14, 1919
Lake Gitano	May 28, 1919
Lake Glasco	June 14, 1919
Lake Fablus	July 1, 1919
Lake Fabyan	June 28, 1919
Lake Fairfax	July 23, 1919
Lake Fairlie	July 30, 1919
Inglenook	Aug 13, 1919
City of Flint	Oct 7, 1919
Detroit-Wayne	Nov 8, 1919
McCreary	Nov 19, 1919
Vinton County	Nov 29, 1919
Hancook County	Dec 2, 1919
Lake Tresa	Dec 9, 1919

Fig. 16

Fig. 17

Fig. 18

Lake Falum . . . . .Dec 12, 1919
Lake Tippah . . . . .Dec 19, 1919
Lake Fandango . . . . .Dec 24, 1919
Lake Fandon . . . . .Dec 21, 1919
Montfaucon . . . . .Mar 13, 1920
Chippewa . . . . .Mar 27, 1920
Ononoaga . . . . .April 9, 1920
Cayuga . . . . .April 22, 1920
Oneida . . . . .May 4, 1920
Mertone Farr . . . . .Sept 11, 1920
James Davidson . . . . .Oct 9, 1920

Fig. 19

Fig. 20

Fig. 21

Figure 18

The Maryland, *one of the largest steamships on the Great Lakes during its time, being launched in Wyandotte in 1890. (Courtesy of the Bacon Memorial Public Library)*

Figure 19

Another view of the Maryland. *(Courtesy of the Bacon Memorial Public Library)*

Figure 20

The Western Star *during construction in Wyandotte. (Courtesy of the Bacon Memorial Public Library)*

Figure 21

The Landsdown, *built in Wyandotte in 1895, was moored in downtown Detroit for some time. It was used to ferry railroad cars across the river from Detroit to Windsor until she blew an engine in 1970. More recently it was a riverside restaurant in Detroit.* (Detroit Free Press)

Early families in Wyandotte used either home wells for drinking water or brought water in buckets from the river. Epidemics of typhoid fever, tuberculosis, and the gradual pollution of the river by industrial deposits brought a need for reforms in the methods of water use. In 1881, an intake pipe was first installed to run water from the river to the fire department. In 1882, water mains were extended to homes. A pumping station was added in 1889. A filtration plant was built in 1918-1920 to overcome the effects of river pollution.

The sewage problem grew during this time also. In the early days, sewage infiltrated the soil and refuse water ran through ditches along the roadways and streets until it found its way to the river. The first steps taken to improve the sewage disposal was the outlawing of wooden drains in 1893. It wasn't until 1907 that a new system was completed. This system used gravity to flow the sewage to the nearest body of water (the river!). A pumping station was added in 1930, to solve a growing problem of backwash of water and sewage in basements. This system included an outlet box that led straight to the river. It was not until 1939, that a modern sewage disposal plant was built. (Long-time mariner Bill Heinrich commented after proofreading this paragraph that "those were my in-the-Trenton-Channel-Days, I wonder how I am still alive!")

Another significant time for most border towns, including Wyandotte, occurred with the passage of the Michigan prohibition law in 1919. This turned out to be an exciting time for nearly all residents regardless of their status or beliefs. The "real action" occurred along the Detroit River. The northern tip of Grosse Ile was said to be bootleggers paradise, as was Gibraltar. An exciting vantage point for the onlooker was the riverside seat of the interurban streetcar as it sped by, just north of Wyandotte. At that time the shoreline had not been filled in, and the tracks for the streetcar ran along close to the edge of the steep bank of the river, which was solidly filled in with boat houses with living quarters above them. Between the houses was scarcely room for narrow plank walkways. This spot was a natural base for the powerfully equipped speedboats of the rumrunners, enabling a quick take-off or return at any given signal. Occasionally an onlooker would catch a glimpse of a government boat in hot pursuit, trying to catch the craft before it reached the safety of Canadian waters, or surprise it on the return trip. The game of tag was a continuous one, but usually took place under the cover of darkness. This area was known as Hogan's Alley and Dingle Park.

Along with steelmaking, chemical production, shipbuilding, etc., Wyandotte is well known for boat, yacht, and rowing clubs. The Wyandotte Boat Club was first organized in 1875. There have been four locations for boat houses or headquarters. The first clubhouse was located on the river at the foot of Vinewood at Bishop Park. Its equipment and building burned in 1903. The American Legion clubhouse became the headquarters in 1923. A shed next door to the Legion building housed the shells. The third boat house was erected along the boat bay in back of the Wyandotte General

Hospital in 1946, on land donated by the Wyandotte Chemicals Corporation two years earlier. The most recent clubhouse is next to the par three golf course on the south end of town. There is great tradition among the rowing community in Wyandotte from the Boat Club's origin. Over the years, the oarsman athletes have achieved high honors and great distinction, including National Championships in 1892, 1928, and 1943.

Some nautical memories Wyandotte residents may recall include watching an airplane carrier pass by them on the Detroit River in 1942. It was the only airplane carrier ever to pass through fresh water. The carrier was the former passenger steamer *Seeandbee*, the largest side-wheel vessel ever built anywhere in the world. The United States government obtained the steamer for airplane carrier training and rechristened it the U.S.S. *Wolverine*. Her staterooms were removed and a flat landing surface substituted. It was used for training purposes on Lake Michigan, near Chicago.

TRENTON

When Michigan Governor Cass negotiated the Indian Treaty of St. Mary's in 1818, he established a white settlement from Ecorse to the mouth of the Huron River. Early settler Abraham Caleb Truax traveled from his home in New York to Detroit, where he became a prominent merchant and built one of the best buildings in the area. By 1818, he sold his fine building erected in Detroit and, along with his wife, built a large, two-story home in what would eventually be Trenton. This may have been a spot Truax observed while fighting nearby during the War of 1812. It was the highest spot on the trail between Detroit and the River Raisin. Since it was near the river, they would be in touch with people passing either by land or by water. The land sloped gently toward the river, where occasional channels led to deeper water flowing swiftly. Grosse Ile was across the river to the east, where there were a handful of early settlers.

Before long, the Truax's home became known as "Traux's," and eventually became "The Tavern." Once a stagecoach line was developed between Monroe and Detroit, their home became "the Half-way House." In 1823, it was officially designated as the polling place for the township of Monguagon.

Following the wreck of the Great Lakes' first steamship, the *Walk-in-the-Water*, in 1821 (as discussed on page 11), her salvaged engine was placed in a new larger ship called the *Superior.* The captain of this ship was proud of her and ran an ad in the *Detroit Gazette* early in the spring of 1823, heralding her proposed runs the coming season. Of course the amount of ice in Lake Erie would affect the actual starting date, but if conditions were favorable, the first run would be scheduled to leave Buffalo on April 25. So confident were the owners of the *Superior*, that they set up a firm schedule for the season. On May 3 and every ninth day thereafter through November 8, she was scheduled to leave Buffalo at 9:00 a.m. for Detroit. The Detroit return departure time would be 4:00 p.m. beginning May 7. The ad further stated that precautions were being taken to assure safe and regular runs. Even duplicate paddle wheels were provided in order to keep delays at a minimum in the event of one being broken.

The original stops between Buffalo and Detroit included Erie, Cleveland, and Sandusky, "unless prevented by stress of weather." A few years later, an additional stop would be added at the little village of "Truaxton." This was the beginning of a community, named after Abraham Truax, that was gaining attention as the mid-point between Detroit and Monroe. And the "Truax's Tavern" became busier than ever with more travelers stopping by and more territorial business being taken care of. In 1834, "Truaxton, in the Territory of Michigan" was duly recorded on the map and became an official village.

During this time, water routes were vital, since most roads were so poor. To get goods to the major market in Detroit from Truaxton by road took a full day or longer, but a ship could carry a much larger load and make the trip in two or three hours. Mail from Washington, D.C., to the territorial capital in Detroit by water and land took as little as eight days. By way of the land route only, it took eighteen to twenty-five days.

Another important family in the nautical history of Truaxton (later known as Trenton) was Giles Bryan Slocum. Raised in New York State, he was a teacher. At the age of twenty-three, he set out on a venture that would send him west to the new territory. He boarded the canal barge system on the Erie Canal to reach Buffalo. The trip took eight days, as the barge was pulled by mules. Passenger fare, including board, was 2 cents per mile. On reaching Buffalo, Slocum decided to continue his journey across Lake Erie to Detroit on the steamer *Enterprise*. It was not the most comfortable way to travel, but in order to save money, he decided to purchase deck passage, at a $3 fee. The trip included two nights and up to midnight on the third.

Slocum explored a bit, first in the interior and around the Black River area. Then he turned back near Truax's, where he noted it to be the only good, high shoreline between Detroit and Monroe. After he was completely established in Truaxton, he went back to the East to negotiate and oversee the purchase of merchandise for a village store. Upon completion of his transactions, he began the long journey back across Lake Erie aboard the steamer *Thomas Jefferson*. As the ship approached the territory, the passengers became more and more uneasy as ugly rumors surfaced from passing ships regarding health problems. By the time the steamer arrived in Detroit, the passengers found it was no mere rumor. Within five months of the founding of Truaxton, a second epidemic

of cholera had hit the area. The first night the ship was forced to dock offshore, and no one was allowed to leave the ship. Throughout the night the passengers could hear the ominous sounds of the death carts rattling along the streets, carrying away dead bodies of the twenty-eight who had become victims of the dreaded disease.

The use of waterways for transportation was gaining in popularity, especially since the great success of the Erie Canal. Mr. Truax, and other businessmen from Truaxton, wanted to make their village a center for river travel. They decided to utilize the low marshy area to construct a canal from Truaxton to the Huron River. Their plan was presented to the Legislative Council at Detroit, where it was approved. Capital stock of $75,000 was set. Their company was empowered to create piers, warehouses, other buildings, and necessary improvements to complete the project. The legislative act also stated that the canal was to be opened to all the public as long as the prescribed duty or toll was paid. The act incorporating the Huron Canal and Manufacturing Company was approved March 28, 1836, stipulating that the canal should be completed on or before April 1, 1841. The plan failed before a single scoop of dirt was dug.

Also during this time, the village name was changed to "Truago." There is confusion as to the reason for the change. Some mapmakers continued to use Truaxton as the designation for the area.

By 1837, Michigan's population had increased to 87,273 from 8,765 in 1820. In 1819, there had been only one steamboat operating on the Great Lakes

(*Walk-in-the-Water*, discussed earlier); by 1837, there were thirty steamboats of the largest size navigating on the lakes. Giles Slocum saw this added traffic as an opportunity to build more docking space. He built several docks in the Downriver area, including at Grosse Ile, Gibraltar, and on the Canadian side.

By 1839, Truago was on its way to becoming an important shipbuilding center. Navigation and further shipbuilding continued uneventfully until 1844, when the village was stunned by a tragic accident. The *General Vance* was a small passenger steamer operating from Detroit to Monroe and onward to Maumee, Ohio. Very early in the morning of June 25, the *General Vance* left a dock in Detroit on its way to Windsor, Ontario, with a full load of passengers. After a short stop, the small steamboat left the dock to proceed on its way downriver to Monroe. Scarcely had she cleared the dock when the high pressure boiler blew up. She sank near the Canadian shore with Colonel Truax as one of the unfortunate passengers.

Colonel Truax's tragic death at age seventy-one shocked his community. His son George, his daughter Sophia, and her husband, Giles Slocum, took over the affairs of the colonel, and turned their attention toward the river and shipbuilding. By the 1840s, river traffic had increased to the point where a number of steamers were stopping at Truago. The *Mazepha*, the *Rhode Island*, the *Erie*, and the *Constellation* were a few of these steamers.

In the early days, the approach of a ship was heralded by devices unique to the particular ship. As mentioned earlier, the *Walk-in-the-Water* had a small cannon mounted on the front that would be fired to signal its arrival. Others could be recognized by a peculiar clunk of their paddles in the water, or some other telltale sound. It wasn't until 1845 that steam whistles were invented and used as signals of arrival because of their individual sounds. Some years later, the *Massassagua* had a whistle that went up and down the scale. This sound became known to everyone along the river.

Of the ship captains who were settling in the Truago area, Captain Wagstaff was among the first and most colorful. It is said his interest took him wherever excitement could be found. In the fall of 1833, word came down from the garrison at Fort Mackinac in northern Michigan that the men did not have enough supplies to last the winter. Many would starve if food and supplies could not be delivered to them. The only means of transport was by ship. By this time of the year, all ships in that area had been laid up for the winter. A prominent Detroit ship builder heard of the plight and had one of his sailing vessels made ready to make the mercy run. He stocked the ship well and hired a double crew to prepare for the worst and sent it on its way. The locals were making open wagers on its ability to make the trip and return by Christmas. With Captain Wagstaff as part of the crew, it returned safely with its white sails billowing in the wind late on Christmas day.

Captain Wagstaff also gained attention in 1846 as the captain of the 300-ton sidewheeler *Julia Palmer*. The *Julia Palmer* was only the third ship to be moved along the land between the head of the St. Mary's River and Lake Superior. The ships had to be dragged or moved on rollers across this portage to pass between Lake Huron into Lake Superior prior to the Soo Locks being built.

During the 1840s, at least nine ships were built in the Village of Truago. They included:

A. D. Patchin	875 ton paddle wheeler	lost in 1848
Anthony Wayne	400 ton	lost in 1850
Telegraph	181 ton	built 1849, sunk 1859 in Lake Erie collision
Sultana	800 ton schooner	built 1847, rebuilt as a barge named Cumberland remained on Lakes until wrecked 1858
Globe	1223 ton paddlewheeler	built 1848, lost 1860
John Owen	250 ton paddlewheeler	built 1845, abandoned 1861
Southerner	500 ton	built 1848, shipwrecked in Lake Erie 1863
Arrow	350 ton	abandoned 1865
Alvin Clark		square-sterned brigantine lost in 1864 storm

The Arrow was the pride of the Truago waterfront. Its normal run was from Detroit to Toledo, carrying both passengers and freight. Many glowing accounts have been written of this beautiful little vessel. In 1849, the Arrow's schedule called for her to leave Detroit every evening at 8:00 p.m., stop at Amherstburg, then continue on her way across the lake to Sandusky. She would leave Sandusky for her return trip at 9:30 a.m., again stopping at Amherstburg at 12:30 p.m., on the return trip to Detroit. The fare from Detroit to Amherstburg was 25 cents. Freight was 12½ cents per barrel bulk.

This little ship gained the reputation of being the fastest steamboat on the western waters. She had not gone unchallenged. In the summer of 1849, it was announced that the Arrow had left Amherstburg with the Empire State and had passed her "handsomely" one mile out in the lake. Later in the summer, she downed another challenger as she sus-tained her reputation for speed. This time it was the Atlantic. The Atlantic had already passed by the Amherstburg dock before the Arrow had even cast off, yet the Arrow caught up to her and beat the Atlantic by several boat lengths before reaching Detroit.

As with all ships, the popularity of the Arrow eventually ran out. After serving in various capacities, she was abandoned and scrapped in Green Bay, Wisconsin, in 1865. Her engine, however, was salvaged and eventually used in two other ships.

Excerpts from Truaxton, Truago, Trenton, include the description of another ship built in Truaxton during this time.

There it lay for 105 years, deep on the bottom of Lake Michigan, keeping its secrets to itself and bothering no one. But that quiet century came to an end one miserably cold day in November, 1967.

Something had snagged the nets of a fishing trawler so badly that a scuba diver was called in to free them. When he found how completely they were tangled in the masts of an old, unknown sunken ship, he had to call in other amateur divers to help.

They found the ship so remarkably well preserved that they wanted to raise her, but every expert consulted, and many who were not, agreed it was too hazardous an undertaking.

The amateurs were undaunted and decided that raising it was worth any danger involved and in July of 1968, they began.

Working 16 hour days, seven days each week, the men pumped out over 60 tons of silt from the sunken vessel. From this, they were able to recover the many artifacts which told of the ship's daily life over a century ago.

On July 23rd, 75 men working 16 hours, finally raised her so that she could be towed beneath a large barge to the Marinette Marine Corporation in Menominee. Three days later, she arrived at her destination.

At the time, she was called "The Mystery Ship," as her identity was in doubt. Now no doubt remains that she is the Alvin Clark, a square sterned brigantine built in 1846, in Truaxton. Accounts claim she sank on July 14, 1864, the result of a sudden disastrous squall. Most of her 18 years were spent in transporting contraband lumber from the National forests to Chicago, where there was much money to be made selling it for the booming building trade.

At the time of the above writing, the *Alvin Clark* was the oldest ship to be found on any of the Great Lakes.

The many ships that were forced out of commission for one reason or another were often just left to drift or sink. Many suffered explosions and onboard fires, which burned to the waterline, with the remaining hull eventually sinking. Others left to drift eventually ran aground, becoming a nuisance and peril to navigation.

The large number of ship explosions was becoming a great concern throughout the country. In 1849, the Commission of Patents reported to the U.S. Senate that there had been a total of thirty-three steamboat explosions. These had resulted in 2,660 lives lost, 2,097 injuries, and $3,990,326 lost in destruction of property. Because of this hazard, it is clear that competent ship's engineers were in great demand and received good pay. In 1836, the rate schedule for a captain was $600 to $1000 for the season. Engineers were paid $50 to $90 per month. A sailor made $16 per month compared to the first cook, who had a monthly salary of $25.

In many obvious ways, the steamboat was an improvement over the sailing vessel, but in addition to the ever-present danger of an explosion, there was the extra cost of fuel for each trip. The cost of running a steamship was considerable. For those ships making regular trips across the lakes, costs included not only fuel cost, but the crew's wages, provisions for passengers and crew, and other contingencies. Total costs were normally calculated at $100 to $150 per day. It was common for a steamship on a regular run throughout the Great Lakes to consume 100 to 300 cords of wood. The man in charge of burning this wood, the fireman, was paid a monthly rate of $18.

Ten years after the Village of Truaxton was renamed Truago, it was again renamed, to its current name of Trenton. The state approved this name change on February 5, 1847. The reason for the change is not clear. One theory is that it was named for the strata of limestone beneath the community, which is "Trenton."

The Detroit and Cleveland Navigation Company was formed in Trenton in 1850, with regular runs between Cleveland and Detroit during the navigation season. This line operated two years with two ships, the *Southerner* and the *Baltimore*, both sidewheelers built in Monroe. The company changed hands in 1852 and commissioned the Turner shipyard in Trenton to build the 479-ton sidewheeler *Forest City*. This was the first of this line of ships to be built in Trenton. Its name was later changed to *Bay City*. It was wrecked at Clay Bank in 1862.

Trenton had gained a variety of industries within the decade, but shipbuilding remained the most important. The *Morning Star* was built in 1862, below town on Front Street, just north of Slocum's Island (now Elizabeth Park). The launching of the *Morning Star* was a big event in the area, with people coming all the way down from Detroit and up from Monroe, eager to witness yet another

steamer being added to the lakes. She was a fine 1,075-ton propeller-driven steamer and stayed on the Cleveland run until colliding with the *Dunderburg* in 1868, near Cleveland.

By 1865, Trenton's population was listed as 1,300 people. By this time railroads had become popular and were in competition with ships for transportation. Ship owners began to add bands and other enticements, such as fine dining areas, to keep their clientele from the railroads. The typical trip from Buffalo to Detroit took three to four days and cost about $10.

During the Civil War days, villagers were kept informed of the battlegrounds and actual fighting through accounts in the newspapers, the letters sent home, and from the men themselves as they returned from their terms of service. Being near the Canadian border made them aware of still other war-related actions, including the underground railroad. In the Detroit area, with the proximity to Canada, there were certain buildings that were known points of refuge for the escaping slaves. Rumor has it that there was a refuge in the Truax homestead in Trenton, where there is an underground space.

Following the Civil War, normalcy returned to Trenton and the surrounding area. One industry that was prospering was the saw mill industry. One mill was located at the foot of Pine Street. Before the arrival of trains in the area, the river provided an easy route for getting the logs to the mills, where they were cut. The sawed lumber was then transported by steamship or barge, if it was to go any distance, or by lumber wagon for short hauls. As winter closed in, making navigation impossible, it was not uncommon to see huge piles of sawdust stretching north of the docks, as well as below, intermingled with uncut logs and piles of finished lumber waiting for the spring navigation season to open.

Most of the time the villagers had to arrange for their own entertainment, but occasionally they were treated to a special event that could be enjoyed by old and young alike. The arrival of the circus in town was just such an occasion. It would come by boat, and everyone in town would be on hand to get the first glimpse of the circus people with all their strange paraphernalia. In 1865, it was the Dan Rice Circus that made its appearance. There was plenty of space for the circus to pitch its tents in the vacant fields between Pine and Maple streets on the east side of Fourth. The young lads eagerly offered to help, doing odd jobs ordinarily shunned, just to get a chance to be in on the excitement.

Carrying sawdust to the circus from the huge piles at the mills was probably one of the jobs carried out by village boys. This by-product of Trenton's main industry at the time did have other and more practical uses as well. The butchers in particular made good use of it on the floor to absorb the blood of animals that they slaughtered. Meat markets used the sawdust into the early 1900s for this purpose. Many butcher shops also had their own icehouses filled with cakes of ice layered with sawdust.

Commercial icehouses along the riverfront utilized sawdust too. Sawdust was lavishly used between each block as insulation for the ice stored in these large, barn-like structures. When the ice

on the river had frozen 18 to 20 inches, or thick enough to hold the weight of the teams of horses and sleds, the men went to work with their huge saws especially made for this purpose. The ice was sawed into blocks and taken into the icehouse and stored in sawdust. When hot weather arrived, the iceman would harness his team and tour the town with his ice wagon, watching for a card in the window of homes, indicating ice was needed for the icebox.

One winter in the late 1860s, the weather had been exceptionally mild, not allowing the river to freeze thick enough to cut ice and fill the icehouses. The men would not be daunted by this turn of affairs, however. They had the local blacksmith make them some long-handled grappling hooks. Then in late spring, the ice from the upper river and Lake St. Clair broke up into large pieces and floated downstream. With the use of these special hooks, and ropes tied around the old pilings of the docks just north of Elm Street, the men would pull in these huge cakes of ice. These cakes would be sawed into squares that would eventually fill the icehouses.

Shipbuilding continued as a major industry in the late 1860s. The *Mary Pringle* was a screw-driven ship built in 1868, at the Turner yards. The owner of this 166-ton vessel was in the business of buying consignments of oak staves to be sent to a concern near Buffalo, New York. To facilitate the loading of the cargo, the owner had docks built at the rear of his Front Street home at the edge of the channel. The *Mary Pringle* continued in use until she was burned near Port Huron in 1893.

The ill-fated *Amazon* was one of the largest and staunchest crafts to be built at the Turner yard. She was fastened together with pegs made of teakwood and had two wheels and a double stern above the load line. She met her fate when she was beached on northern Manitou Island in a blinding snowstorm.

Ships built at the Turner yards include the *Active*, the *Advance*, the *Alert*, and many other schooners that remained in active service for years. At one time Captain Turner employed as many as 350 men building ships. During the eight or so years of his shipbuilding career in town, he constructed at least thirty-six vessels, eighteen of which were steamships. Sometimes there were as many as five vessels in the stocks at one time.

By the 1870s, Michigan farming had increased, large salt deposits had been discovered, and other industries had been developed. Lumbering, however, was still the commercial leader. Around Trenton the local lumber supply dwindled, although some lumber was still brought in from nearby woodlots and groves by horse-drawn lumber wagons. Trenton's location on the Detroit River gave it an extra advantage, for this made it possible to supplement the local supply of lumber with logs floating down the river from northern Michigan and Canada. These logs were guided by trained men with pike poles and perhaps a tug-

boat or two, used in the same way a shepherd makes use of his trained dog. There never seemed enough supervision to keep the most daring of the youths from enjoying that very dangerous sport of log-hopping. Even an expert at the game occasionally slipped and was dumped, only to be caught by other logs as they quickly and mercilessly closed in on their slow but steady course downstream to the mills.

During the middle 1800s, plans were made for a system of railways to crisscross the state. By 1858, there were three railways crossing the state. Trenton had access to the railways for quite some time, but the coming of the Canada Southern Railroad was to have a still greater impact on the township and surrounding area. The railroad was incorporated in Canada in February 1868, and the line to Essex and Amherstburg was completed in 1873. The plan was to continue the line by ferry from Amherst-

Figure 22

Early view of the Michigan Central Railroad Bridge between Trenton and Grosse Ile, completed in 1873. (Courtesy of the Burton Historical Collection of the Detroit Public Library)

Figure 23

Another view of Railroad Bridge from Slocum's Island to Grosse Ile. This bridge was rebuilt into the current automobile "Free Bridge" to/from Grosse Ile in 1931. (Courtesy of the Grosse Ile Historical Society)

burg across the Canadian channel of the Detroit River by way of Stony Island, build a short-spanned bridge from there to Grosse Ile, cross the American channel by bridge to Slocum's Island, then continue on to the mainland. This route would take the line about three quarters of a mile below the village of Trenton, where it would join the Lake Shore and Southern Railroad, which ran north and south. The Toledo and Canadian Southern paralleled the Lake Shore at this point.

Word soon spread of the proposed railroad construction project, and many newcomers arrived looking for work. When the main track was laid between the mainland and Grosse Ile, a side line, or spur, was constructed that curved off and down to the dock at Slocum's Island, making it convenient to load or unload cargo shipped by water. The completion of the project in 1873 connected Detroit to Buffalo by rail. The railroad was a great improvement over boat travel as far as speed and seasonal travel were concerned, although it may have been more expensive.

The railroad employed many men in a variety of areas, including running the bridge itself. The bridge had to be kept in repair, and the mechanism for turning the two channel spans had to have constant attention. This job required two men, each working a twelve-hour shift, seven days a week. These men had to have a good knowledge of the machinery and to be ready to swing the spans so that ships could pass through. They also had to be alert to signal, if there were any incoming trains.

There would be the occasional emergency that the bridge attendants would have to react to. One story ended in tragedy, which the attendant on duty was powerless to prevent. Regular railroad workmen occasionally used handcars to go back and forth across the bridge between Grosse Ile and Trenton. They were trained to watch for trains coming and to watch for the opening of the bridge for ships. One day some young people commandeered a handcar, either to beat the wait for the train or ferry, or for a lark, and started across the bridge. They had failed to notice the bridge was open, and the attendant could not get their attention or get the bridge closed in time to prevent their falling into the fast moving water below. This memory of the handcar careening toward the water with screaming panicked teenagers aboard heading for a catastrophe remained a nightmare for the bridge attendant for many years.

The railroads allowed the shipment of goods by either rail or via the river. During this time, Grosse Ile farmers cultivated large quantities of fruit, which could be whisked off to eastern markets, as could thousands of barrels of whitefish coming from the Detroit River. Just north of Trenton was a huge deposit of limestone. It was so near the surface that it was easily worked by men using picks, shovels, and teams of horses. Along with this Sibley quarry were a number of kilns used for the manufacture of lime. The quarry was also on a rail line, so either the railway or ships could be used to get the product to market. The shipping and rail business became so great, that a tunnel was planned and actually started between the lower end of Grosse Ile and Trenton. It had to be abandoned when it was discovered that the strata of limestone came so near the surface that it made the project too expensive. Limited information found at the Grosse Ile Historical Society suggests that a rail tunnel was also started from Stony Island toward Canada.

Even with the railroad bridge, local travel between Trenton and Grosse Ile still primarily depended on ferries or privately owned boats. Crossing the river was difficult in the old days. Cattle were driven to the river bank to swim across the river tied to boats and canoes. The first ferry boat to cross the river to Trenton was a crude raft that was used in bringing supplies to the island and crops from the island to market. Sometimes horses were carried on the raft, and sometimes they were attached to the end of the raft and made to swim.

This raft was replaced by a horse-powered wooden scow ferry. The side paddles were propelled by a horse revolving about a lever in the center of the boat. The horse walking around and around in the center of the boat provided the power to propel the boat. The wheels would splash and gurgle during the river crossing. Once the river was crossed, news and mail would be collected and delivered.

Spaces were allotted on the ferry for carts, wagons, and horses. Benches were provided for passengers. A horn was used to call the passengers for boarding. This ferry was captained by Alfred Hentig, who guided the horse and steered the craft at the same time. Reverse motion was impossible unless the horse was unhitched and turned about. Horses used on these ferries were useless as plow horses, because they

were unable to hold a straight furrow.

The first ferry operated between Grosse Ile and Trenton at the foot of Pine Street in Trenton and what later became Ferry Road on Grosse Ile. With increased population on the island, a second ferry was established by Sam Dubry of Sibley. This ferry ran from the upper end of the island at Keith's dock to the community of Sibley. The ferry was powered by steam. Ferry boats had many troubles during the winter, primarily with ice jams on the river. Often they were unable to run in the winter and were replaced by horse-drawn sleighs or skates on the solid ice.

The death of the Turner Shipyard in the mid-1870s dealt quite a blow to Trenton. It had been so important to the livelihood of many households, and it left many men with large families out of work. Things began to look a little brighter in 1883, when John Craig left a Gibraltar firm that had been building and repairing ships since 1866 and decided to build his own shipyard in Trenton. He built the shipyard at the rear of his home along the marshy bank of the river. Slips were dredged out of the marshes to accommodate the needs of the business. He did not build a dry dock, but instead used one of the old type marine railways to move the ships. One end of the rail was sunk into the water, and the vessel to be repaired was then centered on it and firmly secured and pulled out of the water to be repaired.

The new shipyard was like a shot in the arm to the village. Again the locals had plenty of work, and others were pouring in from as far away as Maine. The John Craig and Son Shipbuilding

Company was in full production by the fall of 1883. Large timbers for shipbuilding were brought into town overland as well as by boat. The shipyard made all types of ships: the yacht *Sigma*, a handsome boat made for M. S. Smith of Detroit, at a cost of $45,000; the steam barge *Rhoda Emily*; the steamship *Schoolcraft*; the schooner *Ashland*; and a long list of others. On the stocks in 1886 sat a steam barge claimed by Mr. Craig to be the largest to have been constructed on the Detroit River up to that time. It had a 250-foot keel, 40-foot beam, and 25-foot depth. The total estimated cost of this barge was $180,000.

Active	Schooner	335 Gross Tons	1871
Adain	Schooner	62 Gross Tons	1864
Advance	Schooner	366 Gross Tons	1871
Albany	Schooner	283 Gross Tons	1872
Albert	Schooner	360 Gross Tons	1871
Arrow	Steamer	350 Tons	1848
Ashland	Schooner	991 Gross Tons	1886
Bay City (formerly *Forest City*)	Steamer	479 Gross Tons	1851
Canton	Schooner	320 Gross Tons	1873
Dart	Schooner	297 Tons	1850
Dove	Steamer	440 Gross Tons	1867
Elphicke, C.W.	Propeller	2058 Gross Tons	1889
Emily, Rhoda	Propeller	570 Gross Tons	1884
Fick, C. L.	Schooner	89 Gross Tons	1867
Forest City (See *Bay City*)			
Gettysburg	Propeller	1087 Gross Tons	1887
Gilchrist, J. C.	Propeller	1827 Gross Tons	1887
Hale, O. J.	Schooner	326 Gross Tons	1874
Hydra	Canadian Tug	6 Gross Tons	1892
India	Schooner	316 Gross Tons	1873
Iona	Canadian Propeller	284 Net Tons	1892
Jeanie	Steamer	193 Gross Tons	1889
Juno	Canadian Propeller	10 Gross Tons	1880
Keating, A. C.	Schooner	326 Gross Tons	1874
Keys, D. H.	Schooner	183 Gross Tons	1873
Lansing	Propeller	1611 Gross Tons	1887
Mantenee	Schooner	647 Gross Tons	1873
Marks, John	Schooner	299 Gross Tons	1870
Mary Ethel	Canadian Propeller	99 Gross Tons	1879
May Queen	Steamer	688 Tons	1859
Metropolis	Steamer	425 Gross Tons	1863

The completion of one ship at the Craig and Son Shipyard was held up in a rather unorthodox fashion. The story told is that as the ship was being constructed, a pair of swallows decided to make their nest in the bow, where the mother bird proceeded to lay the eggs. The eggs were finally hatched, and the men were given strict orders to stay away and not disturb this young family until the babies could function on their own. Captain James Chase and James Pringles were co-owners of the ship, which was being built for the run between Detroit and Buffalo. Naturally, when the ship was christened, the name chosen was the *Swallow*.

Above and on the facing page are partial lists of ships built in Trenton, from the book, *Truaxton, Truago, Trenton*.

Minx	Yacht	29 Gross Tons	1889
Monguagon	Schooner	301 Gross Tons	1874
Morning Star	Steamer	1141 Tons	1862
Niko	Propeller	1039 Gross Tons	1889
Nozue Bay	Schooner	648 Gross Tons	1872
Patchin, A. D.	Steamer	870 Tons	1847
Peshtigo	Propeller	817 Gross Tons	1869
Prentice, James	Propeller	535 Gross Tons	1855
Reitz, Chas	Propeller	245 Gross Tons	1872
Ruby	Schooner	106 Gross Tons	1874
Schoolcraft	Propeller	745 Gross Tons	1884
Sea Bird	Schooner	115 Gross Tons	1881
Sigma	Yacht	158 Gross Tons	1883
Southerner	Steamer	500 Tons	1847
Sultana	Steamer	800 Tons	1847
Swallow	Propeller	256 Gross Tons	1873
Turner, Alvin A.	Schooner	309 Gross Tons	1873
Vita	Yacht	69 Gross Tons	1888
Volunteer	Propeller	1944 Gross Tons	1888
Chief Justice Waite	Steamer	571 Gross Tons	1874
Westford	Propeller	302 Gross Tons	1869

Other activities were developing along the waterfront. Frank Parent purchased the property at the foot of Pine where the Sleight Mill had been. By 1882, he had established quite a ferry business between Trenton and Grosse Ile. He also encouraged recreational boating activities of the village strategically located on the beautiful Detroit River. At the foot of Pine Street he had erected a three-story building. The ground floor was used for boat storage and livery service, where boats could be rented by the day or week. In season, one could rent a row-boat and enjoy a pleasant afternoon or evening on the river, perhaps stopping at Slocum's Island or crossing the river to the sandy beach of Grosse Ile.

Mr. Parent's many business ventures kept him busy; therefore, he hired other capable men to run the ferry for him.

During the 1880s, Jewel Troungo was on the job ready to take passengers. With the scow securely attached to the side of the ferry, he could transport a carriage, wagon, livestock, or whatever might need to be hauled to the other side. Some of the islanders enjoyed rowing across to shop and pick up their mail when the weather was favorable.

For the benefit of the islanders, a second ferry ran from the mainland at Sibley's to the northern end of Grosse Ile. Side-wheelers were still on the river at this time. Two made their runs in season from Detroit to Monroe or Toledo, with stops along the way.

During the seemingly short summer season, the leisurely trip to and from Detroit, or an occasional excursion to one of the islands, added much enjoyment to the lives of the local residents. The steamer Massasauga left from Gibraltar to Detroit and returned daily, leaving Parent's dock at the foot of Pine at 7:45 a.m. to return at 5:30 p.m. Beginning in May, the steamer Newsboy ran a pretty tight schedule, leaving Slocum's dock at 7:00 a.m. and 1:00 p.m., with arrivals in Detroit at 8:30 a.m. and 2:30 p.m., respectively.

The 1890s for the Trenton area began as a carryover from the preceding decade. Seasonal work was still a way of life for most families. Not only were the ships' captains and their crews home from the lakes, but mills closed and even

in the area to turn out the beautifully constructed boats of mahogany and other fine woods. For years Mr. Church kept the model of one of his favorites in his office, the 65-foot *Ouananiche*, named for a high-jumping inland salmon.

Figure 24

The Purdy Boat Works, located in Trenton, famous for building their Bimini Babies, 18-foot racing boats capable of 40+ mph. They also built luxurious 72-foot yachts. (Courtesy of the Trenton Historical Society)

Fig. 24

the stone quarry at Sibley went down for the winter season. Several of the large steamers found it convenient to lay up along the shore for the winter. There were few better places than Trenton to lay up, because of the channels inside the marshy area. In these channels the boats were free of floating ice and truly had a snug harbor for the winter.

Mr. Austin Church was an influential man serving as a director of the first bank in Trenton. From 1910 to 1917, Mr. Church interested himself in the building of what were called "day boats." On Front Street, just at the foot of Truax, he had constructed a large building in which to build these boats. Railway tracks ran from the inside of the building into the slip, or channel, at the inner edge of the marsh, enabling the boats to be launched quite easily. This shop furnished year-round employment for many skilled tradesmen

More glamour and excitement came to Trenton in 1917, when Gilbert and Neal Purdy opened their boat works. They were known for the beautiful, big yachts, up to 72 feet in length—complete down to the silverware, table linens, and china marked with the yacht's monogram. Not only did they build many of these beautiful and luxurious boats, but others, including the Dodge Brothers' *Delphine*, put into Purdy's for repairs. Besides yachts, the Purdy Boat Works were famous for their "Bimini Babies," 18-foot racing boats capable of 40+ mph, at a cost of $2,800. Their original location was at the foot of Truax Street. By 1920, they needed more space and found it on the site of the old Turner ship buildings on Riverside at Walnut Street. The large wooden structure pictured in Figure 24 shows their new boat-building facility. It is not certain why the Purdy brothers decided to move their Trenton boatbuilding operation to Port Washington, N.Y., but that they did in 1925, leaving the building vacant.

The Purdy boatbuilding yard lay vacant for a year or so until the Davis brothers moved up from Ohio in 1927. They had financial problems nearly from the start and took on a partner named

Fig. 25

Ben Sampson. Together they formed the Corsair Boat Company, intending to specialize in fast 30- to 32-foot cruisers primarily for the Florida market. The Depression changed their plans, and financial difficulty resulted in Sampson pulling out in 1932. The resulting Davis Boat Yard built several 40-footers for the Coast Guard before it, too, went out of business and was sold to Louis G. Liggett in the early 1940s.

In 1917, L. G. Liggett & Son Company expanded their Detroit Boat Works by constructing a building at the foot of Sibley at the creek. Over the years, in spite of damage by fires and tornadoes, cruisers from 30 to 50 feet were built under the expert eye of Louis G. Liggett. His

unique hulls combined with craftsmanship in mahogany made the Liggett nameplate a hallmark of quality. A boat carrying his name may still be seen on the river occasionally.

The plant, which employed from 50 to 250 employees, turned to production of 110-foot sub-chasers during World War II. The tenth and last of the sub-chasers was completed in 1943. At that time, Lou moved the operation to Riverside Drive at the foot of Walnut. He did not continue boat building, but took on sales of Chris-Craft. The building was

Fig. 26

torn down in 1966 or '67, after Lou retired.

The prohibition law passed in Michigan in 1919 created special difficulty for "border" communities such as Trenton. Ohio was still a "wet" state, and the Detroit River was no real barrier to the importation of supplies from Canada. With Dixie Highway running from

Figure 25

The Liggett Boat Works started building 30- to 50-foot cruisers in Trenton in the early 1900s. (Courtesy of the Trenton Historical Society)

Figure 26

This 1906 runabout was one of the first pleasure crafts built by Liggett Boat Works in Trenton. (Courtesy of the Trenton Historical Society)

Detroit south, through the center of town, to Ohio, Trenton had its share of problems between the law and so called rumrunners. The law-abiding citizens were confused, suspicious of their neighbors, and embarrassed by the position in which they found themselves. Some of the young people, who might otherwise have finished high school or gone on to higher education, were lured by the easy money and the thrill and excitement of illegal liquor traffic.

The enforcement officers were kept busy trying to stay honest and enforce the law. A couple of young fellows who were arrested and brought before the justice claimed they had obtained their booze from a Trenton resident who was selling it on Sugar Island. The use of coal cars on freight trains was one way of hiding the contraband. The local marshal boarded one such train and captured a man in possession of 24 quarts of "red eye." Another had 12 quarts of this treasure, but escaped while the officers were checking the river. Here they found a fellow with a gallon of whiskey, trying to hide it under his coat. At another spot, 25 boxes and three barrels of raisin mash were confiscated. Raisin whiskey evidently was accountable for the scarcity of this usually plentiful commodity from the grocers' shelves. Another time the sheriff's deputy captured an automobile, or "booze buggy," with the radiator filled with four gallons of liquor. Such tales are only a sample of the reports of happenings in the area.

The *Border City Star* of Windsor commented on this particular district at one time as being "the lawless nest of the middle west." Many of the boat houses had tiny dance floors, some type of music, and plenty of Canadian draft beer on tap for 25 cents for an 8-ounce glass.

Along the American riverfront there were factories only in the Wyandotte area. The rest of the distance to Lake Erie was marshland, and small grassy islands still bordering the shore with many slips, or passageways, that cut through the shallow water to the shore. There were a number of creeks that drained from the shore into the river. These marshes and creeks were perfect passages for getting the liquor ashore. They were too shallow for speed boats, but this problem was solved by having a small, flat-bottomed skiff, which was towed behind and could easily be maneuvered through the narrow passages and marsh grass by a person who knew the territory. The load could be transferred from the skiff, then taken to Trenton, where the marsh made it possible to take the load up as far as Dixie Highway, with a man walking, hidden by the tall marsh grasses, towing the boat behind him.

During this period the Coast Guard was very busy in the area. They were based at the foot of St. Joseph Street. Sometimes they would find a boat that strayed out of the deep channel and had run into the swamp and become stuck in the weeds. The Coast Guard pulled it out most willingly, then confiscated the boat and the cargo as well. Occasionally one of the Coast Guard boats would be on the losing end and would return with a badly battered hull. In early 1930, the Coast Guard stationed at Trenton made a request to Washington for additional boats and crews to step up pursuit activities against rumrunners transporting their goods across the river on the ice. They said it was hard enough to handle the summer rumrunner boats, estimated at about 750 private boats. The Trenton Coast Guard had seven boats and thirty men stationed at their St. Joseph Street station. The entire river from Lake St. Clair to Lake Erie was patrolled by only twenty-five government boats.

Some of the young fellows who did the most dangerous work in the illicit business worked for the "big boys," loading the boats and running them across the open water, taking large risks and making about $50 per week. This was quite a sum for that day and a big thrill, but small in comparison to the amount made by the fellows who headed the operation, not to mention the risk of being shot or the constant fear of capture and possible imprisonment.

To get the contraband across the water with as little interference as possible, there had to be good communications. A means of signaling on clear nights was a powerful searchlight on the Canadian shore that was used to beam the message across the sky over Grosse Ile. One readily accessible watching post was Step In, a restaurant on Washington Avenue in Trenton, just north of St. Joseph, near the Knaf bakery. The fellows were known to stop in for lunch or a cup of coffee, as they watched the sky for the signal from across the island. When it appeared, they would phone to relay the message, or be on the way themselves.

The area south of Trenton became known as "Slocum's Island," after the early settler's family built a fine home

there. Although the locals all knew that the area belonged to the Slocum family, and that the house was the Slocum family residence, the villagers had come to feel that it belonged to them also. The Slocum family was extremely liberal in sharing this ideal location with all who wished to come and enjoy it. The huge frame house dominated the highest point, as it faced northward with an unhindered view upstream, overlooking the village of Trenton. At the south end of Front Street, a small wooden bridge, just wide enough for a team or horses, stretched across the marshy stream, separating the island from the mainland. On the island, the property was surrounded by a fence, which kept the Slocum horses, stock, and wandering village cattle away from the dwelling. People, however, were always welcome, and various ways were provided for crossing the barrier. The wide wooden fence across the road could be opened to let wagons and carriages through, and there were wood steps over the fence, as well as a turnstile to let people through.

As spring brought warm weather, Slocum Island became a haven, for picnicking and camping. Permission would be granted for the use of the cleared land for ball games. Tents would soon surround the clearing as campers came for a week, two, or for the whole season. With the steamer making daily runs from the dock into Detroit to get people to and from work, and village stores within walking distance, what more could summer residents want?

Besides the family picnics and regular excursions, there were the very special celebrations that were anticipated each year. Church and other organizations took turns sponsoring these special events. The following article in the *Wyandotte Herald*, describing the 1891 Fourth of July celebration, is quite typical:

It was very difficult to be in Trenton last Saturday without knowing that it was the Fourth. The celebration began before daylight on Saturday morning and lasted almost until dawn of the following day. In the morning the Trenton Light Guard Band, the Knights of Labor, and other local organizations marched in a body to Slocum's Island. The steamers Newsboy *and* Daisy *of Detroit brought many pleasure seekers to the island during the morning. In the afternoon, a Detroit orchestra went to the island and furnished music for a merry crowd of dancers. The athletic games commenced at 1:30 p.m. ... More than fifty dollars in prizes was distributed among the winners of games and races. In the evening the steamer* Newsboy *gave a moonlight excursion to Detroit, but left enough people in Trenton to celebrate in the evening on Slocum's Island, where dancing was the principle amusement.*

Bone remains discovered on Slocum's Island indicate that the land may have been used as burial grounds by the Wyandot Indians. It is also known that it was used for a campground for 600 American troops before a battle with British-Canadian troops at the outset of the War of 1812.

One source states that this land was included in the land grant by the United States to Abram Truax for his many years of military service to his country. As mentioned earlier, Sophia Truax, his daughter, married Giles Slocum, one of

the early area settlers. They lived on the island and built the Slocum mansion. Exactly how the land got in the Slocum family is difficult to determine. Giles Slocum may have bought the property from Abram Truax, or perhaps it was part of Sophia's dowry. A copy of the deed to the property indicates that the trustees of the University of Michigan were somehow connected to this land in the early 1800s.

In 1919, the generous gift of this Slocum land was given as a park to Wayne County. It was deeded for the sum of one dollar by Elliott Slocum Nichols, Alice Slocum Nichols Church, and Charlotte Slocum Nichols, grandchildren of Sophia and Giles Slocum, as the first unit of Wayne County's park system. There were two conditions connected with this transaction. The first was that the name would be changed from Slocum's Island to Elizabeth Park in honor of Elizabeth Slocum Nichols, daughter of Sophia and Giles Slocum, and mother of the three grandchildren who deeded the property to the county. The second condition was that Wayne County would dredge a canal around the property. Although the land had always been called an island, it was in fact a peninsula and had considerable marsh land surrounding it. Work was started in December 1921 by Wayne County, which led to a canal 4,800 feet long and 60 feet wide, eventually making the Slocum property an actual 162-acre "island." The Dunbar and Sullivan dredge *Handy Andy* was used for the dredging.

The beautiful forests of black and white oak, hickory, ash, and elm trees, plus the scenic Detroit River flowing by, made this an ideal picnicking spot for local citizens, as well as those not so local. A 40-foot cement boulevard making a one-mile sweep around the island, a 100-foot concrete dock, a 2,400-feet long, 50-foot wide promenade with boulevard lights, and a swimming beach and boathouse, were all part of the improvements that Wayne County made to the park at a cost of over $400,000. A baseball diamond, lawn tennis, playgrounds, and the possibility of a nine-hole golf course were also included in the development of the park, which formally opened July 4, 1923.

The Slocum summer home was converted into a recreation center. Picnic tables and grills were scattered throughout the park for public use, and soon tennis courts were added, with pony rides becoming still another attraction. During the warm summer months, a special delight was the rides along the river being offered on several boats. One of the earlier ones was the *Major Wilcox*, followed by the *Harry Burrell*. One of the last boats to serve the Slocum visitors was the D.Y.C. ferry, which had been refitted with benches along the sides, providing seating for fifty passengers. Townsfolk and islanders alike could hear the approach of the boat from afar, sometimes late into the hot summer evening, as the gay music from the loudspeakers floated across the water. The old Slocum home was destroyed by fire in the late fall of 1975.

While everyone had been busily engaged in watching Slocum's Island emerge into its new role as Elizabeth Park, another type of activity had been

Fig. 27

developing in the lower part of the Slocum property, just south of the railroad bridge to Grosse Ile. In Detroit there was a rising demand for more electricity, as industrial growth began to spread. In January of 1923, Detroit Edison announced that it was beginning construction of its Trenton Channel Electric Plant, to be located on this property purchased at the south end of Slocum Island.

The construction of the Trenton Channel Plant was a big undertaking. The number of construction workers varied from 300 to 600 and were of all nationalities, from Bulgarians and Turks to Americans, who had heard of the construction work and had come in from nearby states to look for jobs. Many of the foreigners spoke only their own languages and knew little of the ways and customs of this country. As World War I was still fresh in the minds of the people, hostile feelings emerged and often caused trouble. Separate bunks had to be

Figure 27

The Slocum Home was given to Wayne County in 1919 to become part of Elizabeth Park, the first unit of the Wayne County Park System It was located on Slocum's Island, which was turned into an "actual island" by dredging the surrounding marshland. (Snug Harbor)

built to minimize tensions. When the Plant was completed in 1924, it was designated as the world's largest electric plant at a cost of $23 million.

In the late 1920s, airplanes were gaining popularity. Between the planes, cars, and trains, boats were being used less

Figure 28

A View of the Trenton shoreline looking north from Slocum's Island in mid-1930s.
(Snug Harbor)

Figure 29

Another view of the Trenton shoreline, where the Riverside Apartments are now located.
(Snug Harbor)

and less for transportation. They became more popular for cruises and/or for recreational use. Trenton became an important place for amateur rowing regattas, as well as a hot spot for outboard motor boat racing. Trenton has a rich tradition continuing to current times, for all types of boat racing, both rowing and power.

GIBRALTAR

Gibraltar shares much of its early history with the other Downriver communities. The early residents were the Indians, known as the Wyandots (also known as Hurons), who were under French control until the British captured Detroit in 1760. The early Indian tribes used Gibraltar as the "Head Village." It was the headquarters for the Council House and International Council Fires. Since the Wyandots were always a leading tribe in the Northwest, the Great Council of the Confederacy was held there, and decisions were made there concerning important items such as peace or war.

The area was called "Chenal de la Presque Isle" on early French maps. This roughly translates into several other names, all meaning "standing or upright rock," or "big or large mass of rocks." The theory is that when Englishmen began to settle in the area, they began to call it Gibraltar, which, in their opinion, was the greatest rock of all. When original land plats were registered for the area, the spelling was "Gibralt**er**." It was not until 1900 that the spelling was changed to "Gibralt**ar**," which is the current spelling.

The Brownstown Treaty was signed in 1807, which opened up the southeastern part of Michigan for survey, settlement, and new roads. West Jefferson Road follows an early trail used by the Indians traveling from Ohio to the north. It is said that in the spring, Indians traveling north with their families left their mares on what is now called Horse Island to foal. The horses would live the summer on this natural-corral island to feed and were picked up by the Indians on their return trip south in the fall. The Indians would stay in the Gibralter area for some time before heading farther south, taking advantage of the abundance of reeds for making baskets, and for the good hunting and fishing.

The well-documented Commander Perry's battle near Put-In-Bay, Ohio, in the War of 1812, has references to Gibraltar Island, as being used as a lookout. There has been a popular misconception by some that it was Horse Island, part of Gibraltar, Michigan, that served as this lookout. The Gibraltar Island referred to in Perry's battles is actually a small 6-acre island, that is part of Ohio's Bass Islands, close to Put-In-Bay.

Following the successful opening of the Erie Canal in 1825, local entrepreneurs had a vision of building such a canal all the way from Gibralter to Lake Michigan. The Gibralter-Flat Rock Land and Canal Company was organized on July 20, 1836, for this purpose. Their plans were to build a canal between Gibralter and Flat Rock, extending on to Ypsilanti, with the ultimate goal of reaching Muskegon, on Lake Michigan. The prevailing thinking and planning at that time, not only in the Michigan Territory, but in the whole nation, was to develop a network of man-made canals as a means of cheap transportation, both for freight and passengers.

The offices of the Canal Company were located on the second floor of the two-and-a-half-story hotel in Gibralter. Two prominent leaders associated with this enterprise were Lewis Cass, former Governor of the Michigan Territory, and Daniel Webster, a renowned orator and national political figure of the time. Lewis Cass, who lived in Detroit, and Webster were invited to Gibralter. Webster made a fiery speech from the hotel balcony extolling the great benefits that would fall on Michigan by building this canal. He made known that he would personally acquire $20,000 worth of Canal Company stock.

The wheeler-dealer promotions offered by the Gibralter-Flat Rock Land and Canal Company actually filled the area with a number of settlers. The Canal Company advertised widely on the potential of the area as a growing major city, and created such confidence in the scheme that lots sold for $5,000 or more. Dredging actually began along the Huron River in Flat Rock before the project failed in 1838. Some of this original dredging is still evident in Flat Rock.

Gibralter, located in Wayne County, was platted and recorded on March 14, 1837, by Peter Godfroy, Benjamin B. Kerchival, and Joshua Howard, all Trustees of the Land and Canal Company. Amos Dunbar became the first Postmaster of Gibralter on October 2, 1837. The office was renamed Woodbury on December 8, 1838, then back to Gibralter on May 13, 1839, and finally to Gibraltar on December 19, 1900.

As mentioned in earlier sections, there were at least 30 steamboats cruising the Great Lakes by 1837. The importance of aids to navigation was becoming more critical as lake travel was increasing. The U.S. Congress appropriated $5,000 on March 3, 1837, to build a lighthouse at the mouth of the Detroit River in Gibralter. It was the termination of a line of lighthouses between Buffalo and Detroit.

Following is an excerpt from a lighthouse inspector's report taken in 1838 regarding the Gibralter Lighthouse:

Gibralter Lighthouse, at the mouth of the Detroit River, on the western channel: This is lighted with eleven lamps and an equal number of reflectors, fixed. It is a new building, and in excellent order, although (in consequence of the severe indisposition of the tender) there had probably been just grounds of complaint for a few days preceding my inspection of the establishment. I am inclined to believe, however, that the keeper is doing his utmost, and will, on his recovery, give perfect satisfaction.

The dwelling is also a new building, of brick, and without fault, except that the cellar required draining, and the chimneys are out of order. To remedy the former fault, it will be necessary to dig a trench of thirty rods, at a cost of thirty dollars, including all contingencies. Weather-fenders, it is presumed, will remedy the latter defect, at an expense of six dollars each; making a total cost of forty-two dollars.

In 1868, Coast Guard records show extensive repairs needed at the original Gibralter Lighthouse. In 1869, it was reported that the dwelling and tower were in very bad condition and new buildings were necessary. In 1871, an appropriation of $10,000 was recommended and on June 10, 1872, it was approved. The new buildings were completed and the dwelling was occupied by February 1, 1873. The focal plane of the new tower was 47 feet above the level of the Detroit River. This new light was then discontinued 1879, and a custodian put in charge of the property. In 1895, the buildings and grounds were sold at public auction and the lantern and iron stairway of the tower were removed.

There is considerable controversy as to the location of this "second" Gibraltar lighthouse, especially among Gibraltar citizens. There is a house with an attached tower located on Adams Street, just behind the south end of Lowell Street, that looks like the remains of a lighthouse. Many locals assume this was the lighthouse. It took looking up some "older timers" who remember that the house on Adams, with a tower, was originally a farmhouse with a raised water storage tank. The tank was eventually enclosed to form the high tower visible today. The tank was kept full by a 400-foot-deep well, and it supplied most of the homes located in the area at the time.

The Gibraltar Lighthouse was actually located on the northeast corner of the intersection of Grandview and Munro streets. Munro Street was called Worsaw at that time. There were actually three lighthouses on the Great Lakes built from the same plans. The others were located at Copper Harbor in the Upper Peninsula and at Maumee Bay at Toledo, Ohio.

Many of the early settlers in Gibraltar arrived by boat. Many came from the east coast by way of the Erie Canal and across Lake Erie. It was the safer method of travel, because of the undeveloped territory, lack of roads, and the Indian threat. Records show some settlers originally came to the east coast from Europe on sailing vessels, taking an average of six weeks to make the crossing.

As with most of the other early Downriver communities, farming, timbering, and shipbuilding became important parts of the Gibralter economy. Scottish shipwrights, French woodsmen, and Irish laborers poured into Gibralter to build schooners. There were three shipyards in operation at one time, and the town was booming. Men, out in the woods, cut timber for the sawmill. Most of the houses took in sailors and workers as boarders, and a two-and-a-half-story hotel was completely full. The lumber provided planks for the ships and material for the basket shop. A coppersmith shop was also in operation. Sand and cement for the shipyards were brought in by water.

One of the shipyards was owned by R. Linn, who was born in Scotland. He came to Gibralter in 1841, where he became a shipbuilder. He was joined in business in 1866 by Captain J. Craig from New York. They became pioneers in building merchant vessels in the area.

Other shipbuilding names during this period (approximately 1860 through 1894) included Alford, Calkins, Clark, and Morgan. The shipyards stretched from Grandview north on the riverfront. Records show at least 23 vessels were built in Gibralter from 1863 to 1882. They included 6 schooners, 11 propeller, and 6 barges, and varied in size from 47 tons to 1,399 tons.

The population of Gibralter in 1873 was approximately 400. A local Business Directory for Gibralter during the middle 1870s lists the following businesses:

Herman Alford	general store & shipbuilder
John Brown	blacksmith
Doremus & Kitcheell	cigar manufacturers
Linn & Craig	sawmill and shipbuilders
E. Seaton	steamboat captain
William Stoddard	collector of customs
E. Sullivan	hotel proprietor
W. Thompson	stave manufacturer
M. Vreeland	lighthouse keeper

At one time, a small steamboat running between Detroit and Cleveland would occasionally stop at Gibralter. By the 1860s regular service had been established. A side-wheeler named *Olive Branch* came through the West (Trenton) Channel on her round trip from Gibralter to Detroit, stopping at Trenton and Wyandotte. Other ships providing local service to Gibralter were The *Princess, Island Queen, Newsboy*, and *Massasauga*.

The many hundreds of people who had enjoyed the boat trips on the *Massasauga* were shocked when news reached them of the disaster that had struck the ship. It was August of 1890 when the crew, as was custom, had gone ashore at Gibralter to have their supper. Fire broke out on the little steamer, and by the time it was discovered, such headway had been made that it was impossible to save it from being demolished. The *Massasauga* was the last ship to provide scheduled service to Gibralter.

Hector Munro, originally from Scotland, first stopped at Sandusky and Toledo, Ohio, before coming to Gibralter in 1879. He had originally been a shipbuilder, but when he came to Gibralter,

he operated his own schooner, hauling freight on the Great Lakes. While living in Sandusky, Mr. Munro sailed to Canada to pick up his wife and sons, who had arrived from Scotland. The oldest son, Daniel, soon had his own schooner, the *Oak Leaf*.

The *Oak Leaf* was built by the Munros in Gibraltar in 1895. She was 93 gross tons, 86 feet long, 24 feet wide, and had a draft of 7 feet. She, along with the schooner *Charles Chamber*, built in Grosse Ile, were the last trading schooners built on the Detroit River.

People obtained their cooking and drinking water from the river, walking out on small docks and dipping up two pails at a time. During the winter, ice was cut from the river and stored in ice-houses for use later in the year. After being cut from the river, the blocks would be hauled up a ramp, loaded on a stone-boat, and hauled to the icehouses. There it was heavily insulated with sawdust to insure it would last until the next winter season. It was usually cut into 2-foot-square blocks and sold for 1 1/2 cents per block.

The following quote from the *Wayne County Courier* dated January 22, 1885, provides some insight into the activities in the area during that time:

Gibralter is once again more aroused to life and shows signs of considerable vigor. The cause of it no doubt owing to the fact the R. W. Linn's shipyard is being put in order for work. The mill and machinery are being put in thorough order; and as soon as the weather moderates, the mill will start up, after a long rest. The new barge building will employ quite a large force of men and the prospects are good for building another soon.

Messrs. Claston and Parsons have opened a stone quarry near Gibralter Station, and expect to do quite a large business in the stone trade. The railroad company is putting in side tracks for them.

Edmund Hall intends making extensive improvements on his river-front during the early spring. He is having a pile driver built for the purpose of sheet piling, and so present the encroachments of the river on his land. This will be a great improvement and one of considerable expense.

Captain H. Alford, the shipbuilder, has contracted to build a scow for Detroit parties.

The following "Memories of Gibraltar" were in the *Detroit News* sometime between 1952-1955. It is a glimpse of Gibraltar by Richard LaFrance, and his reminiscence of the area some sixty years earlier (late 1880s).

On the blue Detroit River just opposite the lower end of Grosse Ile is the very small Village of Gibraltar. From it one can see, across the five-mile width of the mouth of the river, the shore of Canada, and in between the two Tawa Islands, and Hickory and Sugar Island.

The Village differs little from its appearance in the late 1880s except that some buildings have faded away. The shipyards and sawmill, which then employed the men who did not work on the farms, are gone. There was a store and post office, and a combined church and schoolhouse.

Life was slow, simple, the people poor, with little contact with the outside world. The turnpike, a muddy, rutted route between the Villages of Rockwood and Trenton, passed by Gibraltar, a mile away, and a more muddy and worse rutted road made contact with the village most difficult.

The river was the main artery of trade and travel between Gibraltar, Trenton, Wyandotte, and Detroit. A very small steamer, the Massasauga, *made a daily round trip over this route, tying up at night at Hall's dock in Gibraltar. A few passengers, farm produce, lumber, wood products and general supplies were carried.*

This small steamboat, painted a gleaming white, was a thing of beauty floating on the swift current of the river. Children loved to watch it come and go. Its whistle and bell made men and women pause and look at this white swan making ripples at the bow, foam at the stern, and billows of smoke from the funnel as it sometimes glided over smooth blue water, dazzling in the sunshine, and sometimes broke into view through mist and rain. The most beautiful thing in the world it seemed to this four year old boy.

The Massasauga *unloaded in the summer evenings, the fire was banked and the crew went home. Then the shadows came, darkness hid this loved picture and all was quiet in the Village.*

But one night this quiet exploded into a tumult rousing the village with the wild clanging of the ship's bell and shouts of Fire! Fire!

Someone had been careless or something had gone wrong on the boat. The darkness was broken by a flaring red flame, then a roar as fire spread here and there...for a while the shining white...then a browning surface, then a mass of mounting flames.

I stood in awe with my mother some distance, listening to the strange roar of the fire and seeing the figures here and there attempting to fight it. We could see axes falling on the mooring lines as all hope was lost. The Massasauga floated with the current a short distance downstream, caught on the bank of the dredged channel, and burned to the water's edge.

Then I knew my first great sorrow. Something I loved was gone, forever. I buried my face in my mother's apron and wept bitterly.

After the shipyards went out of business, and the lighthouse was not in operation, a handful of people stayed on. The large Hall Farm on it outskirts gave work for some, and of course, the lakes always provided a living to those who served on the boats.

The Edmund Hall farm is an important part of Gibraltar nautical history. Its location is described in a legal abstract in 1900, as follows:

On the north by Webster Avenue, prolonged as a highway towards Monroe as far as the bridge over the branch of Brownstown Creek, called Black Water, [now referred to as Frank and Poet Drain] and on the west and south by the Black Water and Brownstown Creek, and on the east by the dredged channel dividing Horse Island from the mainland, and by the Detroit River.

The Hall residence was a big frame house on the river at the south end of Lowell Street at Grandview. It had a boat house on the water on the south side of a point jutting into the Detroit River. The farm had pastures with lanes running through, where Holstein cattle grazed, with cattle barns in the area of Stoeflet and Adams. Edmund Hall gave employment to many of the local residents at $1 per day. He also had a blacksmith and carpenter shop combined, a carriage house, icehouse, and a granary.

During this time (up to the early 1900s), the area of what we now know as Gibraltar was largely a swampy area, with a population of approximately 100 residents. The description of Hall's property in 1890, refers to "the dredged channel" between Horse Island and the mainland. Edmund Hall owned a dredge, which he used to drain much of the marshland around Gibraltar. Articles in 1885 also refer to "Hall having a pile driver built to drive sheet piling to preserve his water front land." It is a good bet that he dredged the channel between his property and Horse Island in the late 1890s. The rest of the canal system throughout Gibraltar was dug in the mid- to late 1920s.

In the early 1920s, Horse Island, formerly owned by Edmund Hall's daughter, Frances Chaney Strong, was platted and the lots sold as building sites. They were bought primarily as sites for summer cottages. The remainder of the Hall Farm was platted into lots in 1925. Records show small lots sold for $495 up to $5250 for the larger choice ones. The first private home was built on Hall Island in 1923. There was no gas, water, or electricity. The canal was not dredged across from the home until 1928. Bridges were built and the remainder of canals were finished later. Hall Island was originally known as Little Snake Island. The present bridge on Middle Gibraltar Road was built in 1932, by the Wayne County Road Commission.

Another part of the original Hall Farm includes the present Edmund Island, formerly called Big Snake Island. The first private home was built there on the southern point in 1929, by a dentist named Dr. Vasik. The brick home is still standing on that location and is currently owned and occupied by the author of this book!!!

Prohibition was a law to prohibit the manufacture, sale, and use of alcoholic beverages. Various forms of regulation or control over the liquor traffic were adopted from time to time, but prohibition was the most drastic of them all. The 18th Amendment to the U.S. Constitution was ratified January 16, 1919. In accordance with its provisions, it went into effect one year later, January 1920.

During the 13 years, 10 months and 20 days of the Prohibition Era, Gibraltar lived up to the competition offered by its neighbors up and down the shoreline of the Detroit River and Lake Erie. Canada was the Mecca and the open water between Gibraltar and Amherstburg, the challenge.

The Canadian liquor industry and government gained enormously. They were reluctant to cooperate with the United States government in trying to curb bootlegging expeditions to their shores. Hiram Walker and British American Brewing Company boosted their production to peak output. Exporters fixed and controlled the supply. Scotch whiskey, malt extract, gin, and wines were in higher demand than rum. Exporters realized as much as $60 profit per case. A case of Scotch whiskey normally sold for $32 per case in 1920; bootleggers paid $110. The liquor industry became one of Canada's largest revenue sources. Canadian custom officials levied a $9 tax per gallon on exported booze. This could be refunded upon presentation of a receipt by the importing nation. Since the bootleggers, for obvious reasons, were not equipped with the necessary United States papers, the Canadian government did not refund the taxes levied. The Canadian government gained over $30 million for their treasury in 1928 alone.

Following are excerpts regarding bootlegging and rumrunning activities around Gibraltar during the prohibition era from *Gibraltar – Our History*, published by the Gibraltar Bicentennial Committee. For obvious reasons, specific details and names are not included.

It was surprising the number of people living at that time in Gibraltar who had a part in bootlegging in one way or the other. It was necessary to recruit boat pilots, watchmen, laborers to handle the liquor in loading and unloading boats and trucks, drivers to take it out of the community; it took a lot of help. Times were not good and a man had to feed his family.

We asked a resident what a small building on Lowell at the back of the lot was built for, and found that it was built and used as one of the strategically placed lookout points. Before the house and marinas were built on North Gibraltar Road and Middle Gibraltar

Road, you could see when a car was coming and be ready to signal to those engaged in this illegal operation.

The "importing" was done between 1925 and 1932, which were low water years. They had to have river men who knew where they were going to operate the boats at night. One who could by instinct stay in those channels was valuable, because if they got into the wild celery beds, they would back up a couple times and not know which direction to go. The patrol boats would cruise the channels after daylight and tow the stranded boat into Detroit-confiscating both boat and booze.

In one interview we were told of a man who wasn't making money fast enough to suit him by working for someone else; he saved his money and bought his own boat for $1,800, went across to Canada, and bought a load of liquor (he had to pay cash). On the return trip he ran afoul of the Feds., jumped overboard and swam ashore, losing his total investment. It was his first and last experience in big time bootlegging and he then went back to work for the other "importer."

According to what one resident read in the paper, he told how a still was raided in Gibraltar by the Feds. The Detroit News *said it was a $100,000 operation. There was an empty house with a tunnel under the next lots that came out into a basement where the still was located. He mentioned no names or the location of the house. This was all according to what he had read the following day in* The Detroit News.

"Importers" took advantage of the development along the shoreline with boat houses, boatwells, dead end streets and private homes. New structures with outlets to the water and access from land were especially built. Water craft of every description defied the Coast Guard and other law informants agencies. Sleek cruisers with converted cargo spaces took great pains to appear legitimate. Speedboats with hopped-up engines (originally designed for aircraft and light in weight) outran the law. Other bootlegging craft included a "mosquito fleet" consisting of rowboats and canoes with outboard engines. These little luggers would ply in the shallow water where the Coast Guard would not dare venture. Tugs and steamers were built for larger hauls and would plod along at seven knots. A single run could make the "importer" wealthy for life, carrying a $600,000 cargo. Cars were used when they believed the ice to be strong enough to support their weight and, as related to us, many a "bootlegger" was not successful and his car and load would break through the ice and end up at the bottom of the river.

"Rumrunning was a young man's game. It took nerve and good boat handling. You couldn't stop doing it, because if you stopped, and started thinking about what you were actually doing, then you would stop for good," says a rumrunner who had his share of close calls making eight or nine round trips a day across the river. He added "I've never been in jail overnight, and I never lost a bottle in my life."

If a bootlegger sensed imminent capture by the Coast Guard, he had two choices, return to Canada where the Coast Guard could not follow or jump into the water. Sometimes a slow and fast boat would be lashed together. To avoid capture the "rummies" would jump into the faster boat and escape while the Coast Guard overtook the slower craft which was used as a decoy.

This observation was made: "In those days, names didn't mean much. If someone didn't know your name, he couldn't tell on you. If you were a good boater, everyone sought you and you got a lot of protection from people around you." There was a great deal of opposition to this law and, in general, was not a popular law.

The introduction of weapons into the smuggling operations began as an incident in late 1923. A patrol boat captured a booze-ladened vessel. Its ten escorts attempted to sink the Coast Guard boat by ramming. After this incident, all waterborne law enforcement agencies were assigned weapons; service revolvers, sawed off shotguns, and automatic rifles. The smugglers, not to be outdone, armed themselves with submachine guns or any weapon available.

During this period, a bootleg-buster by the name of Torgney Hagglove, Chief Boatswain's Mate in the Coast Guard, began to strike fear into the bootleg operations. Torgney, overcoming internal corruption, uncooperative citizens and Canadian indifference, armed himself with an automatic rifle, coffee and sandwiches. He would lay and wait aboard his fast speedboat for the "rummies" to slink by. Then he would nab

them red-handed, often engaging in gunfights. Between 1928 and 1929, he caught 42 smuggling vessels. An observer said, "Hagglove was a determined person, a real good skipper. Everyone ceased operations when they heard he was in the area. We never knew whom, when or where he'd hit next."

Sometimes the bootleggers would bring beer in burlap bags, 24 bottles to a bag. On occasion, the booty was dumped over side or taken to the back creeks if the law enforcement agencies were closing in on them. Later, fishing expeditions would be underway, not necessarily as interested in catching fish as they were in snagging their dumped booty. Once in a while an innocent fisherman would recover a cache, lift anchor and leave the area as quickly as he could with his lucky find.

Finally, in 1930 the Canadian Parliament passed a law prohibiting the sale of liquor to nations under prohibition laws. It was an end of an era and would never be the same again. During this period of prohibition, we saw the greatest growth of illegal stills along the Canadian border states.

The country eventually tired of the experiment. Congress passed the 21st Amendment in 1933, repealing the 18th or Prohibition Amendment.

Today Gibraltar is well known to many for its boatyards and marinas. The Horse Island Boat Basin was one of the early boatyards. It was started in the early 1920s by Otto O. Rieger, when he constructed a home, store, and docks on the north end of Horse Island. It was sold to the Tenant family in 1958. The City of

Gibraltar bought the property in 1993 and tore down the store building and docks, to make way for the potential replacement of the Horse Island Bridge. The bridge, built in the early 1920s, was declared a "historic bridge" in 1992, the same year it was made eligible for possible replacement by the Michigan Critical Bridge Fund program. There had been studies recommending it be torn down and replaced, but being declared "historic" meant it would have to be preserved. That meant a new bridge would have to be built next to the old one if it were actually declared unsafe. The replacement/rebuild subject became moot in late 1996, when a local engineering firm declared the current bridge safe, with an estimated lifespan of an additional fifty years.

The Chalk Boat Works was opened on North Gibraltar Road in 1939, where Mr. E. Chalk had boat wells, repair facilities, and storage. It is no longer there.

The Gibraltar Boat Yard began in the 1946-48 period by Fred Blakely and Hazen Munro. It originally consisted of about twenty boat wells on the west side of the canal coming into Gibraltar from the Detroit River. They later added a gas pump and a marine accessory and parts store. The marina had grown to fifty-five boat wells when Jack Bulh bought the operation in 1968.

Heinrich Marine (now Humbug Marina) was started in 1954 by E. W. (Bill) Heinrich. He bought the property on Middle Gibraltar Road from Bill Lawson when it was primarily a cattail swamp. After a year or two of dredging, there was room for about 100 boat wells. They sold Chris Craft boats from their

operation at the north end of the island until 1964, when the marina was sold to the current owner, Evertte Hedke, and it became Humbug Marina. As mentioned earlier, the basic canal system throughout Gibraltar was dug during the 1920s. This included the narrow main canal that cut through Gibraltar at a right angle turn from the Detroit River, past the current location of Humbug Marina, and eventually into Brownstown Bay. The original location of Gibraltar Boat Yard and Heinrich Marine was on this narrow canal coming off the river.

In the mid - to late 1950s, the City of Gibraltar hired Bill Heinrich and Hy Dahlka to change the entrance of the main canal off the Trenton Channel, to increase water flow throughout the canal system. They made the original 90-degree canal entrance into the large angled "bay-like" entrance that currently leads into the Gibraltar Boat Yard and Humbug Marina. This change increased the canal water current through Gibraltar from less than one mile per hour to over three miles per hour, and helped keep the canal system clean. They also dredged the entrance to the south end of Horse Island, off the Trenton Channel, currently marked by three sets of channel markers. This project also included dredging the channel between the south end of Horse Island and the main Gibraltar Island, which is also currently marked by three sets of channel markers. The city and Horse Island residents also paid to have Mr. Dahlka dredge along the west shore of Horse Island, and use the backfill to fill in the swampy area, to make it wide enough to build houses on both sides of the street running through the island.

As mentioned, Evertte Hedke bought what is now Humbug Marina from Mr. Heinrich in 1964, and he and his family still run the operation today. During the 1970s, Mr. Hedke and Carl Droege built the first major boat in Gibraltar since 1895. It was a meticulous reproduction of the original 25-ton, 56-foot long steam-powered paddlewheel boat *Suwanee*. The original old pilot house from the original *Suwanee* was installed on the hull built in Gibraltar.

Marine Specialties, where they sold engine parts and did repair work, was started across the main canal from Humbug in 1967 (current location of Damark rack and storage).

Diamond Boat Sales was opened by Jim Diamond in June of 1975. Their original building was once the Gibraltar Bank.

Gibraltar became a village in 1954. One of their first priorities was establishing a sewer system. This was necessary for building subdivisions and supporting what was to become their biggest employer, McLouth Steel. McLouth Steel Corporation built their $19,000,000 cold steel rolling plant in Gibraltar in April 1955. North Gibraltar Road originally passed through the middle of the McLouth property. The City Council passed a resolution in 1961, closing the original road and rerouting North Gibraltar Road to its present location. This provided 409 acres and over half a mile of uninterrupted riverfront property owned by McLouth.

Starting in 1955 or '56 Gibraltar had its own police patrol boat to patrol the canals, looking for boats making damaging wakes or other marine offenses. The boat was a 26-foot Davis with a steel hull. Many stories are told regarding complaints from local residents of the large wakes produced by the patrol boat itself as it pursued the various offenders. The patrol was discontinued in 1958.

In 1961, with a population of 2,187, Gibraltar became the "second smallest" city in Michigan.

Gibraltar was home to the small Boblo Island ferry boats from 1984 until the end of 1993. The large ferry boats to Boblo were out of Detroit, with the smaller boats from Gibraltar and Amherstburg, Ontario, supplementing the main service out of Detroit. The large boats were discontinued from Detroit in 1991, leaving only the small boats supplying transportation to and from Boblo. The owners of Boblo had planned to discontinue service to the island completely from Gibraltar after the 1993 season, with only the Amherstburg boats running. Their decision to permanently close the island amusement park after the 1993 season eliminated all passenger ferry service to the island.

Fig. 30

Figure 30

Gibraltar's police boat, which patrolled the canals from 1955-56 to 1958. (Village of Gibraltar)

Another Gibraltar area that has recently been developed includes the boat ramp on Cherry Island. Cherry Island is just west of Gibraltar, separated by the Frank and Poet Drain System. There were eighteen houses on this island, on the waterfront facing Brownstown Bay. The prime property around these homes was bought by Wayne County's Metro

Park System in the 1960s. The Park System began buying these homes in early 1980s. It was a very trying time for the homeowners, as they were being pressured into selling their homes and threatened with seizure. By and large, most of the property owners did not want to move.

Neighbors felt pitted against each other, as one would sell, leaving even more pressure on those remaining. The last house was torn down in 1991. The residents of Gibraltar fought the construction of the proposed boat ramp in numerous hearings and other legal actions for many years after the plan was made public. Nonetheless, construction of thirteen boat ramps began in 1992. A 30-foot-wide channel approximately 5 feet deep was dug from the boat ramps all the way to the Trenton Channel in 1993. The facility was opened to the public in late summer 1993. Early residents of Cherry Island recall finding many artifacts left over from the prohibition days along the shoreline and the bottom of Brownstown Bay. Low water, or when the water would be washed out completely by southwest winds, would reveal old bottles (some still full), boat parts (props, etc.), coins, and even guns.

Another local (and not so local!) controversy took place in Gibraltar in the late 1980s. Excerpts from *The Detroit News,* dated April 7, 1989, describe the plans for construction of a large marine complex on the McLouth property in Gibraltar.

Plans for a Downriver renaissance with a $300 million marina-hotel-condominium complex along the Detroit

River in Gibraltar appear to be floundering amid warnings that the project will endanger valuable wetlands and wildlife and could pollute the river.

Construction of the proposed 1,600-boat marina, billed as one of the largest on the Great Lakes, would destroy one of the last wooded marshlands along the Detroit River, said the U.S. Environmental Protection Agency and the Fish and Wildlife Service.

As proposed last summer, the Great Lakes Yachting Center would include four all-weather marinas, two exclusive yacht clubs, a 600-boat dry-dock storage area, a 300-room hotel and a lighthouse with an interpretive nature center. The boating complex would be surrounded by upscale condominiums and single-family homes starting at $125,000 each, as well as commercial office property.

There were many Gibraltar residents hoping for such a project and others opposed to such a great change. The environmentalists won out, and the project was discontinued shortly after.

Then again in early 1997 plans were unveiled for a mega riverfront development between Trenton and Gibraltar. Excerpts from *The News Herald* on February 12, 1997, describe this latest project.

A development heralded as "premier in the Midwest" appears to be on the horizon for Trenton and Gibraltar.

Made In Detroit Inc. on Friday made official plans to develop a waterfront resort community off West Jefferson Avenue along the Detroit River in Trenton and Gibraltar.

The Detroit-based development company has proposed a 650-acre development that would include a 600-slip marina, an equestrian center, shopping, a marina, a golf course, an amphitheater, a multiscreen movie theater, and a 350-house development.

Of the 350 homes, 35 palatial houses are planned for Duck Hunter's Island [Humbug Island], *just offshore from the two cities; the rest would be on the mainland.*

The project has been a year in the works, and ground breaking could be as early as August [1997]. *The development could be completed in 1999, according to Gerald Johnson, president of Made In Detroit.*

The article goes on to discuss the environmental impact of such a project. Approximately 433 acres of the proposed 650-acre development is virgin land, including some of the highest quality wetlands on the Detroit River. These concerns must be addressed with the various state and federal agencies before any groundbreaking will begin. As with other grandiose proposals concerning developing the Downriver area, not all of the locals are jumping on the bandwagon to support such a plan. Some are skeptical, and some "like it the way it is."

The residents of Gibraltar and Cherry Island have lived through many floods over the years. Among those remembered, most occurred in 1952, 1972-73, and 1985. Unusually high water, swollen by strong northeast winds, are the combinations resulting in the flooding. The Army Corps of Engineers built stone dikes along the waters' edge throughout Gibraltar in 1973, as a result

of the floods in late 1972 and early 1973. These dikes were several feet high and limited the water view from most houses. They stayed in place for some time, until the wood framework rotted allowing them to fall down, or until property owners tore them down, preferring a better view to the potential protection from high water. The floods in early 1985 convinced most individual waterfront property owners in most of the city to construct berms (clay dikes) along their property. These berms were constructed in 1986, and remain in place.

GROSSE ILE

The earliest French explorers traversing Lake Erie and the Detroit River identified this island as la grosse ile, referring to its grandeur and size. After 1763, due to British influence in and around Detroit, the French article was dropped and Grosse Isle became the accepted name. That version persisted until the twentieth century when, after several decades of perseverance, island residents finally re-established the spelling as Grosse Ile, both legally and in general use.

Grosse Ile was controlled by the French until it became part of the British territory in 1760, as a result of the French and Indian Wars. The Macomb brothers (Alexander and William) received a deed for the island from the Potawatomi Indians in 1776. In making the purchase, the brothers violated British regulations. All negotiations with Indian tribes were supposed to be conducted by the British Crown. In that same year, the Michigan Lieutenant Governor gave the Macombs permission to occupy the island. They built the first homes and began settling the island.

General Alexander Macomb (son of one of the original brothers) acquired ownership of several neighboring islands in 1817, including Hickory, Sugar, Celeron, Stony, Fox, and Calf. Stone was sold and transported by boat to many surrounding areas from Stony Island. Fishing was also a major industry in the early 1820s. Reports of 16,000 whitefish taken in 12 hours were recorded.

The fixing of the actual boundary between Canada and the United States through the Detroit River was a matter of extended negotiations. Due to ambiguity and various possible interpretations, it was not settled until a compromise was reached in 1822. This settlement placed Sugar and Stony Islands in the United States. It defined the channel of the river as being between Bois Blanc and the Canadian shore, and designating the center line of that channel as the boundary, excepting that the island of Bois Blanc should be British Territory.

The canoes of the Indians and the skiffs of the white men coming later were the first means of transportation from the islands to the mainland. Small sailboats were also used in the early days. In the winter, passage could be made much of the time on the ice, which generally stayed strong and solid between the islands and mainland during the cold months. In the open water, or when the ice was floating, a more precarious method of making the crossing was by paddling in small skiffs or "duck boats" with runners on the flat bottoms.

The Great Lake's first steamship, the *Walk-in-the-Water*, would often be engaged by Grosse Ile residents for Fourth of July celebrations, where it would cruise between Lakes St.Clair and Erie. While under way, speeches, dinner, and dancing would be provided. Other early ships visiting Grosse Ile include the schooner *Superior*, which left Detroit in November of 1827, picked up freight in Grosse Ile, and arrived in Buffalo by December.

The only steamship ever built in Grosse Ile was the hull of the *Uncle Sam*. It was built in 1832, at the easterly end of Horsemill Road by the Detroit Monroe and Maumee Steamboat Company and taken to Detroit for completion. It was about 200 tons and was not renowned for speed or safety. It was lost in 1848, at Cunningham's Island.

A two-masted schooner, the *Tom Lewis*, was built on Grosse Ile in 1847. It was nearly 38 tons, with a square stern and no figurehead. It sailed at least until 1859.

Reports of Grosse Ile being part of the Underground Railroad for fleeing slaves is undocumented. There was one incident reported where the custody of three slaves was given to a man who intended to transport them from Detroit to Sandusky by boat. Prior to leaving Detroit, he learned of free and armed slaves on the Canadian side that intended to board and rescue his slaves. He took the slaves to Grosse Ile, planning to load them on the ship there for transport to Ohio. However, the slaves escaped on Grosse Ile, before being loaded onto the Ohio-bound ship.

the fields on the island. It turned out the horse persisted in his habit of walking in a circle, making him a very poor worker in the fields and impossible on a straight road.

Throughout the 1860s, one family held the only ferry license to operate between Grosse Ile and the mainland. There were many disputes regarding fees. The Wayne County Board of Supervisors ended up appointing one arbitration committee after another to hear complaints relative to ferry rates and regulations. By 1867, they had established the following rate schedule:

For each person	$0.05
One horse with wagon, cart or buggy, and one person	0.25
Two horses and wagon, and one person	0.35
Horses and one person	0.25
Each additional horse or colt to above items, or single horse	0.10
Neat cattle, three or less, each	0.20
Neat cattle when more than three, each	0.15
Each hog or sheep, or calf, five or less in number	0.10
Each hog or sheep, more than five	0.04
Wagons, carts, carriages, rollers, mowing machines, etc., when not a team	0.20
Plows and drags	0.10
Bags of grain, potatoes, or anything else, when not the load team, each	0.03
Barrels of pork, flour, salt, or anything else, each	0.10
Passenger's baggage, not exceeding 60 lb. to each person	FREE
Passenger baggage over 60 lb	0.05

The first Grosse Ile ferry to be operated as a business venture started in 1851. It was a primitive affair, powered by one horse, operated for passengers and/or carriages, and landed just north of Ferry Road. The paddles were laboriously worked by a horse continually walking in circles around a capstan, upon which the driver sat. Later when a small steam launch was used to tow the wagon scow, the horse was retired and put to work in

Other rates were established for the winter months.

Discontentment continued for years regarding one family having exclusive rights to run the ferry. By 1871, a license was granted to the "Grosse Ile Ferry Company" to begin a steam-powered ferry. They began operation in 1874, with a crude scow (barge), powered by an attached steam-powered "launch." The launch, being lashed to one side of the scow, made clumsy crossings even in the smoothest weather. At the Grosse Ile landing, the scow was inched upstream to the dock with ease; at the Trenton side, the scow was maneuvered to the landing stern first, so wagons could move forward to disembark.

At both docks, foot passengers had first to walk onto the scow before reaching the launch, sometimes a risky venture. Uncomfortable seats ranged around the craft, seat backs to the gunnels. Life preservers were scattered carelessly about. When it stormed, oilcloth-type curtains were provided. Of all things relative to riding the ferry, the most intriguing was hailing the boatman docked on the opposite side. The ferry never crossed empty unless persistently summoned. There were four means of signaling for service, including:

- megaphone
- banner
- bell
- lantern

Though appreciative of its importance in their lives, few islanders ever became sentimental over the ferry.

An early steamboat named *Brotters* made a daily trip from Trenton to Detroit and back. In 1852, when an increasing number of inhabitants came to Grosse Ile, a boat named the *Pearl* made trips from the east side of Grosse Ile to Detroit. When this boat became unseaworthy, the *Dove* took its place. Landings were made at Major Horace Gray's dock.

Figure 31

Steam-powered ferry running between Grosse Ile and Trenton beginning in 1871. (Courtesy of the Grosse Ile Historical Society)

Steamboat service was also established from Detroit to Gibraltar. Stops were also made in Wyandotte and Keith's Landing on the west side of Grosse Ile. The steamboat would remain in Gibraltar overnight. Boats also traveled to and from Detroit and Amherstburg, Ontario, where they made two stops on the east side of Grosse Ile.

Fig. 31

The *Princess* was a pressure steamboat, with a peculiar chugging sound followed by a whiz of escaping steam. This boat could be heard long before it came into sight, because its boiler eventually became leaky. The fix for this leak was a dose of cornmeal in the boiler each morning before the daily runs would begin. This would carry it through the day. One of the results of this fix, was the cornmeal would end up coming out of the exhaust stacks and being deposited on the passengers. They often arrived at their destination looking as though they had weathered a blizzard.

Around 1870, rumors circulated that a railroad was to be built to cut across Grosse Ile to connect the United States mainland to Canada. Most local residents took an "I'll believe it when I see it" attitude. *The Detroit Free Press* published related articles in 1871. By 1872, a railroad company had actually bought some property for the project. There were many organizations "for" the proposed railroad, and nearly an equal number "against." Many of those opposed to the project were those who feared it would interfere with river traffic along the channel between Stony Island and Canada. By June 1872, the railroad had already hired forty men to begin building a bridge from Grosse Ile to Stony Island. Eventually there would be three bridges built to bring the railroad to Stony Island: one over the canal between the mainland and Slocum's Island, a second between Slocum's Island and Grosse Ile (over Trenton Channel, current location of the county "Free Bridge"), and the third going from Grosse Ile to Stony Island.

Studies were conducted regarding the feasibility of either a bridge or tunnel being built to connect Stony Island with Canada. Neither proved to be practicable, so the Canada Southern Railroad Company embarked on the only other alternative. They ordered a railroad ferry be built at Jenking Shipyard, in Walkerville, Ontario, with completion scheduled for January 1873. It was not until May that the *Transfer* would be launched. The launching was a gala affair, with hundreds of people witnessing the christening. It was the largest vessel ever built west of New York. It weighed over 2,000 tons. She was a double-ender, having a rudder at each end; she could navigate either end first. Being a side-wheeler equipped with one engine on each wheel, the *Transfer* was exceptionally maneuverable. There were three tracks on her 244-foot deck, holding up to twenty-one railroad cars (smaller cars than used now!).

After a trial run early in June, the crew expressed satisfaction with the vessel; they were pleased with her "behavior" and the "efficiency" of her machinery.

Fig. 32

Fig. 33

Her huge proportions and fine appearance when under way attracted admiration along both sides of the river as she proceeded late in July from Walkerville to Amherstburg for duty. This "mammoth car ferry" was put into service in September 1873, carrying railroad cars to and from the Stony Island dock and a ferry slip at Gordon, Ontario, two and a half miles north of Amherstburg.

Figure 32

The "double-ended" Transfer, which was used to transport railroad cars between Stony Island and Canada from 1873 until 1888. (Courtesy of Burton Historical Collection of the Detroit Public Library)

Figure 33

The Michigan Central Railroad located at the corner of Grosse Ile Parkway and East River Road, current location of the Grosse Ile Historical Society. (Courtesy of Jim Engle)

Once this series of bridges was complete and ferry service had begun, Grosse Ile hummed with railroad activity. Structures built along the railroad right-of-way included an engine house, machine shop, blacksmith shop, and customs house. A brick depot building was built just south of the tracks near East River Road (current location of Grosse Ile Historical Society). A cattle yard was established on land now occupied by the Grosse Ile Country Club. Here the cattle were unloaded for rest and refreshment, and to await processing through customs. A variety of hotels and boarding houses sprang up along the way to provide homes for the railroad employees.

This rail line continued for about ten years. Sometime after 1883, the Michigan Central Railway purchased and merged with the Canada Southern branch, allowing a more direct run to Detroit. This caused regular ferry service between Stony Island and Canada to be discontinued. However, on the few occasions that ice would block the Detroit-Windsor route, the ferry would run between Stony Island and Canada. This continued until 1888, when the Stony Island ferry service was discontinued for good. The bridge between Grosse Ile and Stony Island fell into disrepair after ferry service was discontinued, and the last spans were removed in 1913, following the construction of the Livingstone Channel. The stone abutment at the east end of Grosse Ile Parkway that once supported the bridge is still evident today, as is the peninsula that extends west off Stony Island that shortened the distance between the two points.

The Michigan Central, however, continued to run a daily train to Grosse Ile to accommodate the islanders for school and business. In 1924, the influx of automobiles made this run unnecessary, and rail service to Grosse Ile was permanently discontinued.

The chart inside the front cover shows Grosse Ile and Trenton as they looked during the 1873 to 1883 period when the railroad bridges were in place. This very interesting chart shows which canals and islands are natural.

Following the closure of the rail bridge between Trenton and Grosse Ile, there was fierce argument before the Grosse Ile Board of Supervisors over the proposition to provide one or two free automobile/pedestrian bridges to Grosse Ile. Members organized the Down River Free Bridge Association, to boost the idea of purchasing the old rail bridge and converting it into a free automobile bridge. Opponents of the purchase claimed "Michigan Central wants $75,000 for its bridge, which is so decrepit that it has been condemned for railroad use." They went on to say "the railroad bridge is not a good proposition, it is condemned, is only 12 to 15 feet high, and is junk."

After wrangling over the matter for weeks, the County Board of Supervisors voted to purchase the railroad bridge for $75,000. They also estimated that from $200,000 to $500,000 would be required to place the bridge in shape for use and to connect it with the highway on the end of Slocum's Island.

Excerpts from the *Wyandotte Herald* on August 21, 1931, include:

The village of Trenton and the townships of Monguagon and Grosse Ile are making elaborate preparation to celebrate the dedication of the new county free bridge to Grosse Ile on Thursday, September 3, 1931.

In the morning there will be a water carnival sponsored by the Wyandotte Boat Club. At 10:45, there will be a surf-board riding contest. Riders equipped with long poles will endeavor to push other riders from their boards. Plenty of fun and excitement is promised by this program.

From 11:30 am to 2 pm, there will be outboard motor races. It is expected that some world-beaters will be among the contenders. Cash prizes amounting to $100 will be offered, as well as eight silver cups. Men from Selfridge field will be present to give an exhibition of stunt flying.

Opening of the new bridge will remove the last barrier to free access to any place in the state of Michigan.

Prior to the opening of the Free Bridge between Trenton and Grosse Ile to automobile travel, a "Toll Bridge" had been built between Riverview and Grosse Ile sometime earlier. The motive for this bridge being built is not entirely clear, but it seemed to be promoted by E. W. Voigt. He owned most of the north end of Grosse Ile. As far back as 1890, rumors were circulating that he was investigating plans to build such a bridge. Talk of these plans caused much concern to many residents both of Wyandotte and Grosse Ile. Excerpts from the *Wyandotte Herald* on September 20, 1890, express some of these concerns.

Mr. Voigt owns the head of Grosse Ile, extending as far south as George Alexander's property. By throwing this property open to easy access with the mainland, he could divide the property into lots and sell it off at good stiff prices. In case the bridge is built, it is intended to extend the electric car service of the Wyandotte and Detroit River railway to the island.

Before a bridge can be built, it will of course be necessary to get the sanction of Congress, a requisite that may not be easily forthcoming. Then, too, it is a question whether Grosse Ile culture will take kindly to the idea of being invaded by the vulgar outside world. A bridge with plebeian street cars running over it is something quite likely to send cold shivers down the backs of the island's exclusive set. So, that brewer Voigt's mercenary scheme to increase the value of his land may encounter a bad frost in the home of its inception.

This article refers to Voigt as being a brewer, as he did own a brewery in Detroit. This adds to part of the folklore for his wanting to build a bridge. He raised horses on the island to pull his brewery wagons. The only way he could get his horses back and forth to Detroit was to ferry them across the river, thus making the idea of a bridge even more appealing.

Definite plans were being made in the 1909 time frame for a toll bridge to be built between Riverview and Grosse Ile. Many Trenton residents were opposing this bridge, wanting it to be a free bridge, built from Trenton instead. Their plan included selling bonds to finance the project, which eventually failed.

A syndicate consisting of E. W. Voigt, James Ducey, P. N. Jacobson, Cameron Waterman, F. A. Schulte, Otto Reinvaldt and Wallace Brown was formed to finance the toll bridge. Jacobson became the primary promoter. Opinion still differed as to who was actually behind the whole operation. Speculation included someone intending to build a big park and pleasure resort on the island once the bridge was complete. There was even a rumor that the government was going to move the fort at "Fort Wayne" onto the island.

It was not until 1912 that actual work began on the toll bridge. It was reported that Grosse Ile real estate was already feeling the effects of the proposed bridge by this time. Several big land sales had been made, and streetcar tracks around the island were part of the proposed improvements. The bridge was completed in November of 1913. Excerpts in the *Wyandotte Herald* on November 28, 1913, reporting on its opening include:

The new bridge furnishes the 2,000 people, who live on the island year round, their only dependable outlet. The structure is 2,000 feet long, 23 feet wide (one foot wider than the Belle Isle bridge), and cost $200,000. Until spring, the bridge will be open in the daytime only. The officers of the company which control the bridge are: E. W. Voigt-President; F. A. Schulte-Vice President; Ora B. Taylor-Secretary; and Henry P. Borgman-Treasurer.

Controversy continued regarding the toll bridge long after it was completed. As early as 1929, Wayne County negotiated to buy the bridge. The owners were asking for $415,000, plus assumption of a $190,000 bond issue. The County Road Commission recommended against purchasing the bridge, especially since the "old railroad bridge" was being rebuilt for free pedestrian and vehicle travel.

The County Board of Supervisors ordered drastic cuts in the toll charged by the toll bridge, to become effective January 1, 1930. The round trip toll for a car was to be reduced from 50 cents to 25 cents, and each passenger from 6 cents to 4 cents. A toll ticket that could be bought in advance for 20 cents for a car for a round trip was to be reduced to 17 cents. The bridge owners failed to lower the tolls by the deadline, causing still more controversy.

The opening of the free bridge in 1931 brought competition, which forced the toll bridge owners to adjust tolls on their own. They did not actually reduce the rates from those forced by the County Board, but they had to start charging each way, rather than one way as a round trip. The new rate schedule became 15 cents for car and driver one way and 3 cents for each additional person. Toll tickets cost 9 cents each way. By this time, of all of the original toll bridge backers, only Mr. Reinvaldt was still in the area. He and toll keeper Casper Petoskey had been running the bridge since its opening in 1913.

Controversy continues. Talk began around 1940 that the bridge should revert back to the county, since the original thirty-year bond indebtedness would expire in 1942. In fact, the Grosse Ile Township Board passed a resolution in 1940 eliminating the toll charges. Again in 1943, a circuit judge ruled that the toll

Fig. 34

As mentioned earlier, Grosse Ile originally consisted of the mainland and several smaller off-shore islands within the river system. The largest part of the main "Grosse Ile island" is actually

Figure 34

View of Grosse Ile toll bridge after being hit by the freighter John T. Hutchinson *in 1965.* (Wyandotte News Herald)

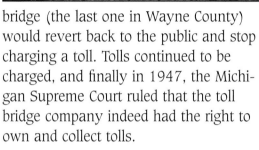

bridge (the last one in Wayne County) would revert back to the public and stop charging a toll. Tolls continued to be charged, and finally in 1947, the Michigan Supreme Court ruled that the toll bridge company indeed had the right to own and collect tolls.

The toll bridge has operated relatively controversy free since 1947. Major mishaps occurred in 1965, and again in 1992, when freighters hit the stationary east span. The Freighter *John T. Hutchinson* hit the span in 1965, knocking two cars into the river. No one was hurt in that incident. The 730-foot freighter *H. Lee White* hit the same structure on September 6, 1992. No cars or pedestrians were involved in the latest collision. The repair cost was put at $1.7 million. The latest controversy surrounds the investigation as to who was at fault for the freighter hitting the bridge. Some reports claim the bridge attendant was late opening the bridge, and others claim it was error on the part of the freighter and/or the tugs who had him in tow. The bridge was last advertised "for sale" in 1981, but not sold.

Fig. 35

Figure 35

Another view of Grosse Ile toll bridge after being hit in 1965. There were several damaged vehicles, but no serious injuries. (Wyandotte News Herald)

two islands, separated by the Thorofare Canal. Originally this canal was described as "simply a marsh; water came in at one end and went out at the lower end—it was not running water, just a marsh." It was dredged and somewhat straightened in 1895 to form the current canal, which still cuts completely through the island. It runs diagonally from the east shore of Grosse Ile just north of the Grosse Ile Lighthouse, to the west shore just north of the Free Bridge. It is navigable to smaller boats in normal water levels, although height is limited by low bridges.

The very north end of Grosse Ile is called Hennepin Point. It also is an island, formed by a small canal separating it from the main island. Hennepin Point is primarily man-made, from industrial wastes deposited since the 1890s by what is now BASF in what was a shallow marsh area. They still own most of the 280-acre island and it is posted "NO TRESPASSING." In 1971, a large sinkhole developed in the middle of Hennepin Point, caused by the collapse of empty salt cavities under the fill. The salt cavities were created by extensive salt mining operations 1,400 feet below the surface. The sinkhole is now full of water, creating a challenge for the guards to keep kids from using it as a swimming hole. There has been no dumping in the area since the mid-1980s. Plans as late as 1969 called for the area to eventually be turned into a major park and marina. More recent zoning ordinances allow no changes to be made in the land until environmental studies at all levels of government have been completed.

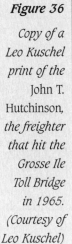

Figure 36

Copy of a Leo Kuschel print of the John T. Hutchinson, the freighter that hit the Grosse Ile Toll Bridge in 1965. (Courtesy of Leo Kuschel)

Fig. 37

Figure 37

View of Grosse Ile toll bridge after being hit by the freighter. H. Lee White *on September 6, 1992.*

Fig. 38

Figure 38

Another view of toll bridge after being hit for the second time. There were no vehicles or pedestrians involved in this mishap.

Figure 39

The H. Lee White *docked at McLouth Steel after hitting the Grosse Ile toll bridge in 1992.*

Fig. 39

One of the larger islands making up Grosse Ile is Hickory Island. It is located at the southeast part of the mainland and is one of the few "natural islands." It has been a popular spot since the early 1900s, having its own beach, dance pavilion, and softball diamonds. Elba Island is just north of Hickory Island on the east shore.

Swan Island is one of the smaller mainland islands, located on the west side, near the south end. It was formally known as Snake Island until it was drained and filled for development. It was a swampy area before the canal separating it from the mainland was dug in the early 1920s. It is named for the Swan Family, who were early residents.

Frenchman's Creek begins at the south end of Grosse Ile, and it extends north past the Ford Yacht Club, before it turns northwest. It forms Round Island, which is south of the airport. It is uninhabited and owned by the Ford Yacht Club. Frenchman's Creek was originally dredged during the early 1920s. It is currently navigable from Ford Yacht Club to the north all the way to Groh Road. It was recently dredged again in 1990, to make it more navigable in low water times. It passes by one of the earliest famous attractions on Grosse Ile, the "Wonder Well." An article in the *Wyandotte Daily News* in the May 19, 1936, edition describes this attraction.

One of the major attractions in the Downriver area which annually attracts thousands of visitors from nearly every state in the Union, is the Wonder Well, on Grosse Ile.

The well produces a natural flow of 2,000,000 gallons of water daily. It has the largest natural flow of any artesian well in the United States.

The water traveling from the ground through an eight inch pipe throws water 15 feet high. The overflow is used to generate all power used at the plant of the Grosse Ile Mineral Spring Company, which owns the well and bottles the water for home consumption.

Fig. 40

The well was drilled in 1903 by an oil company [looking for gas!]. At a short depth water was struck. Drilling continued until the 2,375 feet depth was reached and the gigantic well was struck. For a time the well produced a flow of 4,000,000 gallons daily, but the size of the piping was reduced.

The Wonder Well water has the highest mineral content of any mineral water in the United States that is palatable. Water from the well has been approved by American Medical authorities. Distribution points have been established in Detroit, Wyandotte, Monroe, Battle Creek, Port Huron, Pontiac, and Cincinnati, Ohio.

Visitors are welcome to visit the well any day during the week. The office is open from 9 a.m. to 9 p.m. each day.

Figure 40

The Wonder Well located next to Frenchman's Creek on Grosse Ile. It was a major tourist attraction from the early 1900s to the 1950s. At one time it had the largest natural water flow of any artesian well in the United States. (Courtesy of Jim Engle)

On a recent Sunday more than 3,000 visitors were at the well. Water is bottled in various sized containers for home and office use.

The well was owned by Donald Swan, whose family name was used to rename Snake Island to Swan Island. Don's sister was Isabella Swan, author of *The Deep Roots,* a book on the history of Grosse Ile (often used as a reference for this book). The following excerpts are from *The News Herald,* dated October 5, 1994, just after Mr. Swan's death.

Inventor and chemist Donald Swan, 92, died October 1, 1994, quietly in his Grosse Ile home.

Mr. Swan's well, a major tourist attraction in the area from the early 1900s to the 1950s, flowed steadily until a few days before his death, when it went completely dry. "It literally dried up the week of his death," Mr. Swan's son said. "It's really ironic."

Mr. Swan was an avid football fan, creative innovator, and inventor. He was once interviewed on a national television show as one of the oldest living ex-University of Michigan football players. As an inventor, he was best known for the creation of the smoke bomb. He developed the smoke bomb in the 1970s, after being arrested for selling illegal fireworks in his shop near the Wonder Well. These smoke bombs became important to auto makers for wind-tunnel testing, fire departments for training, and other important uses.

Grosse Ile was the home of another inventor, although not many people have heard of him. With the thousands of outboard motors currently in use in the Downriver area, few boaters know the inventor of the outboard motor was a Grosse Ile resident, and that it was first tested along the Trenton Channel. Excerpts from the *Ile Camera,* dated October 26, 1984, describe events surrounding this great invention.

The outboard inventor was Cameron Beach Waterman (1878-1955) who was born on West Lafayette [in Detroit] and spent his summers on Grosse Ile. His dad owned approximately 222 acres on Grosse Ile's west side, between Horsemill and Church Roads.

Fig. 41

C.B. WATERMAN

Fig. 42

It was February 1905 when C. B. Waterman was in Yale Law School that the story of the first outboard begins. C. B. had ordered a chain-drive Royal Motorcycle, one of the first built in the

Figure 41

Cameron Beach Waterman (1878-1955), who invented the outboard motor while living on Grosse Ile. His first trial was on the Trenton Channel in 1905. (Courtesy of the Grosse Ile Historical Society)

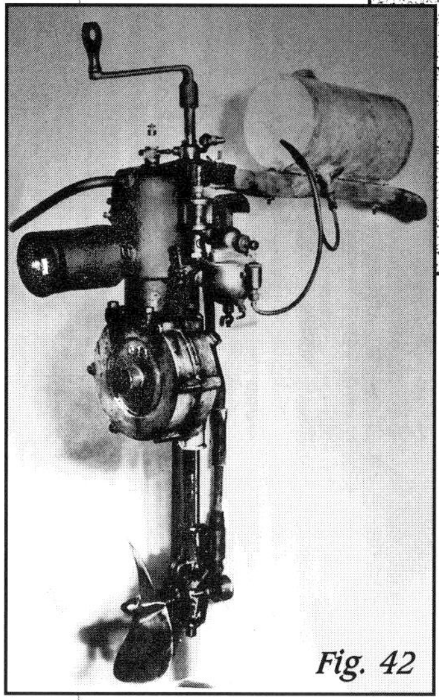

Figure 42

C. B. Waterman's first outboard motor invented on Grosse Ile. He eventually sold his outboard interest to the Evinrude Company in 1917. (Courtesy of the Grosse Ile Historical Society)

United States, to ride around New Haven, Conn. Let C. B. tell the discovery himself, as he did for a boating magazine in the 1950s:

"In September 1903, when I laid the cycle up for the season," Waterman said, "I hung it over the back of a desk chair in my room to clean and overhaul it. It was a four-cycle, air-cooled motor that weighed about 20 pounds.

"As I reassembled the engine, it occurred to me that if I could hang it on the back of a desk chair, I could just as well hang it on the transom of a rowboat and, if a propeller were attached to it, it would drive the boat.

"My next thought was, if I hinged the engine to the back of the boat, it could be used to steer the boat as well as propel it."

Waterman, in his mind, added a tiller and mounted a gasoline tank near the tiller to make the whole thing a self-sufficient unit. He also figured on tilting up the engine to horizontal position to protect it in the absence of a keel or skeg.

He put all of these ideas into sketches later that year. Waterman continues his story...

"My experimenting that fall didn't stop there. I wanted to see how the motor would behave lashed over the back of a chair. In those days, gas illumination was the most common kind. I had a student lamp with a glass chimney, Welsbach mantle and a rubber hose leading to a gas outlet in the baseboard. The Royal motor did not have a carburetor but a primitive predecessor called a mixing valve. I detached the tube from my lamp and fed it into the mixing valve.

"After some experimenting to get a combustible mixture, the little engine suddenly started up."

Waterman graduated from Yale Law School in 1904 and joined the Detroit law firm of Whittemore, Hurlbert and Whittemore. The firm specialized in patents and trademarks.

He dug out his sketches and showed them to his boss, James Whittemore, who asked: "Have you made one yet?"

That led to the manufacture of the first model by a friend in his Detroit machine shop. He wrote to Glenn Curtiss who was building a light air-cooled motorcycle engine and got a three horsepower engine.

In February, 1905, C. B. Waterman and friends took the working model to Grosse Ile, anxious to try it out in the Detroit River. It was attached to a 15 foot rowboat. The tryout was a complete success ... except ice got caught in the chain causing it to slip off the sprocket. That day, the party gave it its name, "outboard motor."

Waterman then formed the Waterman Marine Motor Co., built several experimental models and then 25 more to see how it would sell. By 1907-08, 800 to 1000 motors were produced.

Waterman said his motto was "make a motor boat of any boat in five minutes."

Parts—the motor and shaft—of that first engine are now in the Dossin Great Lakes Museum on Belle Isle. According to Dossin officials, the early engines are brought from storage for exhibition at the Detroit Boat Show intermittently.

Where was that first outboard tested? The Waterman farm was located on Grosse Ile's west side, between Horsemill and Church roads. So the testing occurred in the channel between Grosse Ile and Trenton.

The Waterman farm was sold by 1955.

By 1916, eight different firms had entered the outboard motor field. Waterman sold his entire outboard interest to the Evinrude Company in 1917.

Besides the outboard motor, there was another first for which Grosse Ile is famous. The world's first all-metal dirigible (blimp!), the ZMC-2, was built at the recently completed Grosse Ile airport in the late 1920s. The usefulness of the dirigible was short-lived, so the idea was abandoned. In fact, only one ship was built! The large checkerboard hangar built for its construction remained in place until being demolished in 1960. The roof of the building was moved to the mainland, where it became the roof of a bowling alley on West Road in Trenton. The airport was built on the south end of Grosse Ile, on property once owned by the automobile giant, R. E. Olds.

Fig. 43

Figure 43

The world's first all-metal dirigible was built at the Grosse Ile airport in the late 1920s. The project was short-lived. The hangar where it was built was torn down in 1960, and the roof was moved to Trenton, where it became the roof of a bowling alley. (Week Ender)

AMHERSTBURG, ONTARIO

The history of Amherstburg becoming a town is tied directly to the history of Detroit. As mentioned earlier, Detroit was controlled by the French and later the British, before being taken over by the United States. The upper Detroit River area passed from French to British control in 1760. Detroit was awarded to the newly formed United States from the British by the Treaty of Paris in 1783, although it was controlled by the British until 1796. The British realized the importance of replacing their fort in Detroit with another in an equally strategic location on the river. The search began as early as 1784 and ended up in 1795, when the current location of Amherstburg was chosen as the spot for a new fort to be built.

This was a strategic location, since there were few roads in the area. All commercial and military supplies had to be shipped within a few hundred yards of Amherstburg when entering the Detroit River. There was good anchorage in the channel, and the shoreline was high enough to support wharves and other military needs.

The British prepared to move their Detroit fort to Amherstburg during the year prior to their actually vacating Detroit. They floated some materials from Detroit down the river to Amherstburg in 1796 and began building temporary structures. By 1797, numerous buildings, including blockhouses and storehouses, were complete. This complex was originally known as "Fort Amherstburg," but soon became "Fort Malden."

The fort also contained the King's Navy Yard for the upper Great Lakes. It was constructed just south of the fort, north of the growing town of Amherstburg. It contained storehouses, timber yard, saw pit, and a pier. The navy yard built and repaired ships for the Provincial Marine. All sorts of ships were built, ranging from small open boats to large full-sized three-masted ships. The four most famous ships built were the *General Hunter, Queen Charlotte, Lady Prevost,* and the *Detroit.*

Fort Malden fell into a state of disrepair in the early 1800s prior to the War of 1812. Peacetime economics did not provide the money necessary for basic repairs. However, the declaration of war by the United States on Britain, on June 19, 1812, provided the impetus to get the fort back into shape.

News of the war reached Fort Malden several days following the declaration of war. Shortly after this, on July 2, 1812, the British scored one of their first successes of the war from this fort. The American schooner *Cuyahoga* was sailing from Lake Erie, up the river, past Fort Malden, loaded with supplies. The occupants of the ship did not know of Washington's declaration of war. It did not take long for the startled Americans to give up to a British force that rowed out to meet them from the fort. A bonus for the British was the discovery of papers on the ship outlining various plans for attacking Fort Malden.

Forces from Fort Malden were involved in many battles with U.S. troops in succeeding months. The most famous took place near Put-In-Bay, Ohio, on September 10, 1813, where Captain Robert Barclay led six vessels from Amherstburg to engage Oliver Hazard Perry's nine-vessel fleet. This battle was precipitated by Perry's fleet cutting off the British supply route across Lake Erie, which ran the troops at Fort Malden out of supplies, threatening starvation. The British troops were sent to break the American blockade. Many books have been written about this famous American naval victory.

The loss of the British fleet near Put-In-Bay left Fort Malden defenseless against the American troops. The fort and all government buildings in Am-

herstburg were ordered destroyed, rather than let them fall into American hands. By late September 1813, the Americans entered Amherstburg and began rebuilding the fort near the old fort site. The peace treaty signed in December 1814 gave control of the area back to the British on July 1, 1815. The fort was only partially complete by that time. The naval yard had been burned and rebuilt in the Georgian Bay area, farther away from any future American threats.

The fort again became dilapidated until a Canadian rebellion broke out in upper Canada in 1837. Between 1838 and 1840, there was a massive building pro-

Figure 44

*Early drawing of Amherstburg showing riverfront activities including shipbuilding during the early 1800s.
(Courtesy of Department of Canadian Heritage: Fort Malden National Historic Site)*

Fig. 44

gram that completely revitalized the post. This was only temporary, and by 1851, the last active troops were removed from this historic old post. A plan was put in place to build cottages on part of the fort property to house retired British soldiers.

These "older men" would replace the troops being reassigned, since they were reliable and still capable of performing light military duty. This money-saving plan was in effect until 1859, when all guns and ammunition were removed, which marked the end of the military phase of Fort Malden.

Later in 1859, Fort Malden was converted into a provincial insane asylum. The original twenty or so patients were pressed into action to help repair the again deteriorated buildings. Within a few years it became the home of about 200 invalids and was considered a model for patient care. By 1870, the site was considered too small for the growing needs and was closed as an asylum.

By 1875, the fort property was divided into lots and sold off at a public auction. Many of the buildings were used as a planing mill. Other structures were used for lumber storage and workshops. Items such as window frames, doors, furniture, and even coffins were produced there. This continued through the turn of the century until 1918, when the entire operation was sold to an individual, a previous mayor of Amherstburg. He had one of the large brick barracks dismantled and rebuilt into three separate homes. Other buildings on the fort grounds were demolished. He died in the 1940s, with the property looking more like an estate than a fort. About the only visible feature from the original fort was

the earthworks on the north side of the barracks.

The history of Fort Malden is the heart of the history of the town of Amherstburg. The frequent construction activities and demands for goods and services by the troops attracted private merchants, tradesmen, and others. The majority of the men in town were employed in shipbuilding prior to 1812. Their subsequent homes, shops, warehouses, and wharves located along the river became the nucleus of the emerging town.

After returning to British control from the Americans in 1815, the immediate future of Amherstburg looked bleak. The King's Navy Yard was no longer there as a major employer, when also hurt by many supporting industries, such as ropemaking, etc. By 1818, things began to pick up. Warehouses and wharves began to line the waterfront, making it easy for commercial ships to stop and pick up farm products such as tobacco, wheat, and corn. Most of the commercial shipping was done by sail during that time, with the exception of the steamboat *Walk-in-the-Water*, which regularly traveled between Buffalo and Detroit, often stopping at Amherstburg. By 1820, the town had a population of approximately 500 people, with nearly half being of French descent. The remainder of people were either descendants of the English and German founders, newly arriving British emigrants, descendants of original native inhabitants, or an increasing number of black emigrants from the United States.

The original lots divided in Amherstburg were granted with severe restrictions. The lotholders did not have the rights to will or transfer ownership. This was remedied in 1819, when the government notified the townspeople that they would be able to receive grants similar to other towns, where true ownership would be established. The complete town was surveyed in 1820, with each lot numbered and streets named as they are known today.

Commercial development continued along the waterfront. Merchants began to settle along the river, and more houses were built. Residents continued to graze their livestock on the cleared garrison grounds north of town. Limestone was quarried within two miles north of town. The limestone was sold as a building material and processed into lime by heating it in the lime kilns. Lime was a valuable commodity, being used by tanneries to remove hair from skins and by sail makers to whiten their sails. By the 1830s, residents continued to work in the shipping industry as mariners, dockhands, or providers of food and lodging for passengers and crews of the many ships stopping along the waterfront. One of the cargoes being shipped out of Amherstburg was large quantities of whitefish. The Detroit River yielded bountiful harvests of fish.

By the 1840s, the town was alive with waterfront activity during the shipping season. Amherstburg merchants owned four large schooners, which were used to transport many items, including wheat, corn, potash, tobacco, oak staves, hides, lumber, etc. It took about a dozen hands with a captain to sail these ships across Lake Erie and through the Welland Canal.

Commercial sailing traffic up the Detroit River was difficult because of the current and prevailing northerly wind. It was not uncommon for fleets of sailing ships to be waiting at the entrance of the river for favorable conditions for their chance to make it up the river. During the wait, which could be days, the crews and passengers took advantage of Amherstburg's hospitality in their inns and taverns.

Steamers were becoming popular in the late 1840s. The steamer *Earl Cathcart*, built in Malden in 1846, ran between Amherstburg and Montreal. The *Arrow* traveled between Detroit and Sandusky, picking up passengers in Amherstburg. Daily regular passenger service was established to Detroit and Chatham. By this time, steamer service was common between big cities on the Great Lakes. A trip between Buffalo and Chicago could burn 600 cords of wood each trip. They could not carry that much wood, so they would stop at intervals to get 100 cords at a time. These fuel stops also benefited Amherstburg, as passengers and crew would go ashore to get wood from the wharves and visit the inns and taverns. Travel by land in the area was very uncomfortable, compared to travel by steamer on the river. It was about an hour and fifteen minute trip to Detroit aboard a steamer.

The economy of Amherstburg was further enhanced in the early 1840s when a local merchant, John McLeod, began operating the town's first sawmill. By 1845, the enterprise, known as Malden Mills, was housed in a five-story building located on the waterfront. The equipment was powered by a thirty-horsepower steam engine that did everything from cut logs to grind flour. He also began operating a distillery and rectifying house on his property by 1849. He was an early entrepreneur. He even made his own barrels to store the whiskey. As if this wasn't enough, he also had a shipyard on his property, where he built sailing and steam vessels. One of his ships, the *Thomas F. Park*, was the first vessel to sail from Chicago to Liverpool in 1860. He sold his distillery to Hiram Walker in 1874. Five years later it burned to the ground.

Life continued relatively unchanged into the 1860s. A stagecoach ran between Amherstburg and Windsor daily. The steamer *Pearl* left Amherstburg at 7:00 a.m. daily and arrived at Windsor and Detroit in time for passengers to pick up passenger trains. The wharves continued to be busy, with steamers stopping for fuel, supplies, and passengers as they toured the Great Lakes. Huge coal piles were located along the river, as coal was becoming the fuel of choice, replacing wood. Agricultural implements, such as plows, cultivators, and corn-shellers, and tin and iron works were being manufactured in the area and were common items being shipped out. Many residents were engaged in occupations geared to the shipping industry, including custom officers, saloon/innkeepers, ship's cooks, and many sailors.

Amherstburg found itself involved in the American Civil War in the early 1860s. Windsor became a center for Confederate agents and sympathizers concocting schemes to attack the North from their convenient location in the neutral country of Canada. One such

scheme involved hijacking a steamer, *Philo Parsons*, a side-wheeler, during its routine trip from Windsor, through Amherstburg, to the Lake Erie Islands and Sandusky. Three thousand Confederate soldiers were in custody near Cedar Point, Ohio, in 1864. The only naval Union vessel in Lake Erie to protect these prisoners was the U.S.S. *Michigan*, which patrolled the area around Cedar Point. The Confederate plan was to hijack the *Philo Parsons* before it got to Amherstburg, where sixteen to twenty Confederate sympathizers would be smuggled aboard complete with hidden arms. They would later drop off most passengers and crew on Middle Bass Island and wait for a prearranged signal to attack the *Michigan*. Little did they know that the Union had learned of their plan and had captured the would-be conspirators who were supposed to provide the attack signal. Once it became apparent that their scheme was doomed, they brought the *Philo Parsons* back to the Detroit River, where they abandoned and attempted to sink her at Fighting Island.

The steamer was salvaged and towed back to Detroit for repairs, where it was put into service on Lake Michigan in 1866. It was eventually involved in another historic event, when it was burned at its berth during the Great Chicago Fire of 1871.

Besides being a haven for American deserters and Confederate agents, Amherstburg also had its share of Union sympathizers and heroes.

As mentioned earlier in the Grosse Ile section, a major event affecting Amherstburg residents in the 1870s was the opening of the Canada Southern Railroad in 1873. Initial proposals included building a bridge or digging a tunnel to connect it to the railroad already in place on Stony Island. These plans did not materialize, so ferry service was set up to move the cars across the river from the mainland to Stony Island. The railroad had a major impact on Amherstburg's economy, resulting in the development of residential lots and many commercial endeavors, including lumberyards. It was a primary connection to the U.S. lines until 1883, when the railroad was rerouted into Windsor. It stayed in limited operation until 1888, when all service to Stony Island ceased.

In the early years, most of the Amherstburg citizens got their water directly from the Detroit River. Other than the few who had their own wells, most would buy their water for twenty-five cents for two barrels in the summer and twenty-five cents for one barrel in the winter. It was dipped directly from the river and could include fish, bugs, seaweed, or whatever else might be floating down the river! The water was transported in tanks on two-wheeled carts drawn by horses, filled at the foot of Murray and Gore streets.

In 1891, a waterworks tower was built at the site of the old King's Naval Yard. Water was drawn directly into the tower from the river. Sewage and other contaminants were increasing in the river water from upriver residential and industrial locations. Typhoid fever became common among the local citizens. They began to add chlorine to the water in the storage tank, but it did not stop the annual spring outbreak of the dreaded disease. Boiling the drinking water became the recommendation before the purification plant went into operation in 1920.

During the early 1900s, lawn bowling became a very popular sport in Amherstburg. Many greens were constructed, and as the bowling club membership increased, even more greens were added, drawing people from all over Ontario. A tournament was held each August, where the highlight of the final night was a moonlight cruise along the Detroit River.

The operation of Boblo Island was important to the economy of Amherstburg over the years. In the early 1900s, Boblo was used mainly for family and church picnics and other recreational events. The island was open daily during the summer season, but only for a few hours, closing at 6:00 p.m. Liquor was forbidden on the island during these early years. Many U.S. firms would have annual picnics on the island for their employees and families. Often these outings, which began with the ferry ride from Detroit to Boblo, included a quick ferry ride to Amherstburg after some of the adults became bored with the company picnic. They would take advantage of the hotels and inns, where they could get their fill of local alcoholic refreshment. This was a boon for the local economy and resulted in many tipsy visitors being hauled back to the island, only to have to get aboard the larger steamers for the ride back home.

Free passage of Canadian citizens to the United States without immigration papers ended in 1940, when the Americans decided there was a threat of "undesirables" entering by way of Boblo. This had an immediate negative impact on the ferry service between Amherst-burg and the island. It took some time and negotiating, but finally both sides agreed to a plan that would again allow travel between Amherstburg and Boblo.

After Boblo began adding amusement rides and restaurants, travel aboard the big ferries from Detroit picked up daily during the season. The ferry schedules included dropping passengers off at the island and stopping at the Amherstburg dock on their return trip to allow shop-pers to board and go to Detroit for a few hours of shopping. The shoppers would then ride the ferry back to Amherstburg as it came back to pick up the last load of amusement park guests.

Boblo provided several hundred jobs for young people each summer that it operated. Many successful local profes-sionals earned their college money by working the concessions and restaurants each summer.

The Roaring Twenties brought a Yacht and Country Club to Amherstburg. It was built along the riverfront on the Henry Duff property, which extended from Duff to Brunner avenues. It was the idea of Grant Duff, who received financial back-ing from several Detroit millionaires. One of the backers happened to own the largest Hudson Motor Car dealership in Michigan, who also happened to have one of the largest yachts in the area.

The old Duff homestead was remodeled in 1928 to become the new International Yacht and Country Club. It was of Span-ish architecture and was complete with a large dining room and several smaller private dining rooms, lounges, dressing rooms, lockers, and showers. There was also an open deck on the second floor

where members could relax and watch activity on the river or look out over an eighteen-hole putting course on the 183-acre parcel. Large yachts came by river and docked across the street. The mem-bership consisted primarily of people from the Detroit-Windsor area, although there were some locals. The operation never reached its potential before being destroyed by fire.

The U.S. prohibition era from 1920 through 1933 provided many Canadian citizens with an opportunity to take advantage of their proximity to the bor-der. There have been many stories told and written about "bootlegging" and "rumrunning" during that time. Techni-cally there was a great difference between the two. Rumrunning was the legal export of alcohol to foreign coun-tries from Canada, which somehow got diverted to the United States. That's why all of these government shipments were addressed to Cuba! On the other hand, bootlegging was actually the illegal sale of booze in Ontario.

A section in the book *With The Tide* describes some of the activities surround-ing this rumrunning and bootlegging during that period, many related by the late Walter Goodchild. Following are excerpts from this book:

In those days, Ontario was also sup-posed to be dry, but residents could order liquor for their own use from the province of Quebec. It was surprising how many residents took advantage of this opportunity. So much that large stocks of liquor were built up in garages and basements. These caches were in turn sold to bootleggers who either turned the grog back into the local trade, or shipped it over the river. This should not be confused with the legal export of liquor to other countries. In the case of booze that went over Amherstburg docks, it was all consigned to Cuba.

Not to be outdone by American bootleggers, several local gangs went into the act. Walter was a member of the then famous "Blood and Guts" gang. These young men specialized in highjacking loads and they gathered in many a dollar. One of their hits was at the home of a Colchester Village resident who had a large supply of booze.

The theft was investigated by the Provincial Police, with the result that several young bloods, including Walter, were arrested and charged. The case drew a lot of attention. The trial was held in the second floor auditorium of the Amherstburg town hall, with a packed house. Presiding magistrate was William McCormick, clerk of the town of Amherstburg. At the conclusion of the trial, he found the defendants guilty and sentenced them to ten years in Kingston Penitentiary, along with ten lashes. In comparison to other sentences of the time, this was cruel and unjust punishment.

As young reporters we covered the trial. When my father, the late A. W. Marsh read the story, he remarked, "There's something wrong here. Your job is to check and find out the reason for this unfair sentence." Check it we did and discovered some interesting facts. Our facts were sent to the Federal Minister of Justice and the sentence was shortened. ... It was too late to avoid the lash, however, and the spirit of the young men was broken. None got into any further trouble.

Another story:

Joe Fleury lived at the corner of Gore and George streets and across from him lived Henry Odette. One day Joe called Constable Carl Farrow of the Provincial Police Detachment and reported that his neighbor across the road was bootlegging. "How do you know?" asked Constable Farrow. "I know because he's taking all of my customers" answered Joe.

And another! This one describes the beginning of a local establishment known to all Downriver boaters.

This particular tale concerns Alexander K. Duff, a son of Henry G. Duff and Mary Cunningham, early Amherstburg area citizens.

Coming back from overseas following World War I, Alec got into the bootlegging business. He opened the Deerhead Club on the west side of Sandwich Street, a site now covered by General Amherst High School. Being very successful there he decided to move downtown where he opened a club on the second floor of the building known as Bulluck's Tavern, northeast corner of Dalhousie and Murray Streets. The club was set up, also a hiding place for the liquor, and Alec prepared for a grand opening. A few hours before this event took place however, the Provincial Police raided the premises and went directly to the hiding place. Alec never knew how the liquor was discovered. It so happened that a young man working for him at the time had asked for a raise in salary, which Alec refused. Irate, the young man went to the police and gave them full information.

Later, Alec moved his operation to the Fraser Building, southwest corner of Gore and Dalhousie. Here, because of his political influence, he was able to open a bar and also establish a restaurant in the adjoining building, which provided him the proper regulations for a liquor license. He soon tired of operating the restaurant but continued operating his tavern.

He eventually changed the name to Duffy's Tavern, which he later sold to Zarko Vucini and Mike Jojich. After selling the tavern, Alec moved into an apartment in a small building adjoining the tavern and did a little bootlegging business on the side just to keep in practice.

So this is how Duffy's Tavern, a local social landmark, began!

Another Downriver landmark on the Canadian side is the Seagram's V.O. distillery, just north of Amherstburg. The U.S. prohibition had a great deal to do with its beginning also. It was originally built in 1928, specifically to supply the whiskey-hungry American appetite. It opened in 1929 under the name of Pioneer Distillers Limited. There was even a small airport built close to the plant to facilitate shipment to the United States. It eventually became part of Calvert Distillers. The original plant burned to the ground in 1950. It took three years for the decision to be made to rebuild the plant at its original location. It was rebuilt to be one of Canada's most modern distilleries, with its primary product being Seagram's V.O.

Much has been written about the steamer *Tashmoo* (including pages 20-22 in the **WYANDOTTE** section of this book). She

was built in Wyandotte and launched in 1899. She plied the Great Lakes and rivers during her life carrying thousands of passengers and earning a reputation of being one of the fastest side-wheelers ever built. Her last hurrah ended in Amherstburg in 1936, where she sank, apparently after hitting a submerged rock leaving Sugar Island. The following are excerpts from *With The Tide* that describe that event:

Shortly after midnight on June 18, 1936, we were awakened by the ringing of the bedside phone. It was the police calling to inform us that the passenger steamer Tashmoo *was sinking at the Brunner Mond dock.*

We lost little time in getting dressed and away in the car, all the while envisioning a panic-stricken crowd clawing and fighting to survive. Upon reaching the Brunner Mond bridge we saw the Tashmoo *lying at the dock. Her lights were out but the band was playing. There was no apparent evidence of anything serious.*

Parking at the side of the road, we walked down to the coal dock where an entirely different picture presented itself. The vessel was moored to a platform dock and a wide wooden plank had been raised between the platform and the second deck of the steamer. Assisted by members of the crew, the passengers were disembarking quietly. Some fourteen hundred young people, most of whom were feeling no pain and were unaware of the danger, milled around the dock, built bonfires and one had the impression of a very large, happy beach party. A half hour after the last passenger was ashore, the vessel settled to the bottom, leaving only the upper works above water. The quick thinking and maneuvering of Captain Donald McAlpine and his brave crew had saved them and it was a miracle that the boiler didn't explode.

The Gene Calloway Band didn't stop playing until all danger was past. We interviewed George Moffit manager of the band. He said that the had been in the office talking with the ship's officer at the time of impact. He said, "The band doesn't play while the boat is going through the shallow Sugar Island channel. We went to find out what had happened and when we went below deck found water rushing in. I went up and told the band to play and keep playing regardless of what happened. They kept at it for over an hour after the lights went out."

The Tashmoo had been chartered for a Moonlight Cruise that particular evening by the Pall Club, a Hamtramck social group. She left the dock at the foot of Griswald at 9:20 p.m. for Sugar Island downriver from Grosse Ile. At 11:20 she started the trip back to Detroit and when coming out of the Sugar Island Channel struck a submerged rock which punched a hole in her hull. Water poured in faster than the pumps could handle it. Captain McAlpine ordered full speed ahead to the Amherstburg shore. About ten minutes after the initial shock had vibrated through the ship, she was moored at the Brunner Mond coal dock.

Much has been written about the Tashmoo—i.e., where she was built, some of her escapades, etc...but we are concerned here with the incident mainly because of its happening in our commu-

nity. While the vessel was settling in eighteen feet of water we mingled with the crowd, trying to get a cross-section of the merrymakers to comment on their near-tragic end. None seemed to realize the seriousness of the situation. Many said that they didn't know what had happened until they were on dry land. The main concern seemed to be how they would get back to Detroit. One lad said, "I'm in a terrible jam! I have to be on the job at 6 o'clock...and how will I ever explain to my girlfriend's old man for keeping his daughter out all night?" One of the entertainers, Mrs. Babs Drouillard, worried that she had a six-months-old baby alone at home. Her mother was to stay with the infant until 2:00 a.m., but would then leave confident that her daughter would be home shortly.

Lloyd Brown of Amherstburg was on duty at the Brunner Mond filtration plant when he saw the Tashmoo coming into dock. Sensing that something was wrong he told David Brown, his relief-man, to look after the plant while he went out to the dock to investigate. Lloyd made fast the lines of the boat, moved the improvised gangplank to the second deck, and helped the passengers off the sinking vessel.

Once they were safely ashore came the problem of getting the people back to Detroit. Captain McQueen in his tug Progresso arrived on the scene, as did the Coast Guard boats, and a conference was held aboard the tug between Captain McAlpine, C. F. Bielman, manager of the Tashmoo, and W. W. Subner, representative of the insurance company. It was decided to have the Boblo steamer

Columbia *come down and pick them up. As the* Columbia *couldn't tie up at the Brunner dock, it was necessary for the passengers to walk down to the Boblo Dock at the foot of Murray Street in Amherstburg.*

During this period there was talk of war. Imagine the consternation of the residents along Sandwich and Richmond Streets when their sleep was interrupted in the wee hours on the morning by fourteen hundred boisterous folks marching down the street. They thought the enemy had invaded Amherstburg.

Figure 45

The Livingstone Channel Lighthouse after being hit by the 552-foot freighter E. J. Kulas *on a foggy day in September 1952. (Wyandotte Herald)*

It wasn't until the next morning that most of the town found out what had happened. The passengers thought it was a great joke and carried on with huggin' and kissin' and all sorts of antics. Going aboard the Columbia *they thought it was the end of a gala occasion. The parting shout from some of the merrymakers as the* Columbia *pulled away from the dock was, "Alright folks...we're going home so you can roll up the sidewalks and put out the lights!"*

The police officers on duty that fateful night cannot be given enough praise for their quiet and efficient handling of the crowd. They were Provincial Constables Mullholland and McQueen, Chief Joseph Taylor, Constable Farrow of the RCMP, Constable Harold Brush of Ojibway and S.E.M.

Taylor, Collector of Customs for the Port of Amherstburg.

The Pike Salvage and Wrecking Company of Kingston got the contract to raise the vessel but failed to do so and after many weeks of work had only accomplished stripping the super-structure off the hull. McQueen Marine Limited was awarded the contract to raise the hull on a "no-cure, no-pay" basis. Work began and after many weeks the actual raising of the hull began. It was found that a lot of water was coming in through cracks and other

Fig. 45

small holes, so a wagon load of manure was brought to the scene, which was spread around the hull and sucked into the holes. It swelled and did the job. Later the actual raising began, and as the hull began to come up, there was evidence of cracking, so Captain

McQueen sent over to the Ford Marine Division in River Rouge for a huge pump. As the pump was being lowered under his direction, with the Captain standing below, one of the chainfalls broke. He never blinked an eye but carefully lowered the pump into the hull and in a matter of hours up she came. It was towed to Horseshoe Bay at the north end of Bois Blanc by the tugs Progresso, Henry Stokes *and* Patricia McQueen. *After examining for safety, it was towed to the scrapyard in Windsor.*

Many local residents obtained souvenirs from the Tashmoo...*these were sold by the Pike Company. Irving Kelly, marine reporter for the Westcott Marine Reporting Agency, which had an office in Amherstburg, obtained a pair of deck chairs in perfect condition. Following his death these were given to us by his son, Rev. James Kelly. Father Kelly said that it was his father's wish that the chairs should come to us. They are now in the Marsh Collection.*

Another interesting shipwreck occurred in the shipping channel just north of what is now Crystal Bay. The Livingstone Lighthouse used to stand at the entrance to the Livingstone Channel when approaching from the north. It stood there until a foggy day in September, 1952, when the 552-foot freighter *E. J. Kulas* rammed it, knocking it nearly over. An article in the *Wyandotte Herald*, dated December 14, 1952, describes this nearly fatal event.

Skippers of ore ships on the Detroit River keep their fingers crossed when they pass Livingstone Lighthouse—or what's left of it.

They hope the 900-ton structure, now standing in the channel like a tired drunk, won't topple. If it does, it will block the channel.

- *All this is the result of an argument the lighthouse had with a ship. One man who'll never forget it is E.J. McGuire. He was there.*

- *McGuire is a veteran "marine reporter" who logs ships from a radio shack on the lighthouse platform.*

- *It was exactly 7:30 a.m. when McGuire saw the massive bulk of an ore ship looming out of a pea soup fog and heading for the lighthouse. He screamed a warning.*

The next instant, the Kulas, *loaded with 13,600 tons of ore, smashed into the lighthouse, her bow riding up on the platform. The lighthouse teetered on its base and McGuire's radio shack slid into the water.*

"She knocked it over like it was a matchbox," said McGuire.

"When the radio shack sank," said McGuire, "the suction pulled me under the water. I came up about 100 feet away from the wreckage.

"I managed to swim to the lighthouse, but I was afraid to get back on. It looked like it was ready to go any minute. I would have been trapped under 900 tons of concrete. All I could do was crawl up on a broken slab.

"Meantime, the Kulas *had dropped anchor. She had a hole in her bow plates and was taking on water. The current carried her 600 feet downstream.*

"The captain radioed the dock that

he'd hit the lighthouse. A friend of mine, listening to short wave, heard the ship's call.

"He jumped into his outboard and started looking for me. He got lost in the fog, hit a breakwater, bashed in his hull, turned around and hit the Kulas, *then finally got his bearings and made for the light.*

"I kept hollering to guide him. He picked me up and took me to shore. I had a gash on my head and minus four front teeth."

The Kulas, *McGuire found out later, had lost her bearings in the fog because her radar had conked out. Engines barely turning, she was drifting with the current at eight knots. After the crash, she got her pumps going and went on. Nobody on the boat was hurt.*

This wrecked lighthouse was replaced by a new one. The crib (foundation) for the new one was put into place in October 1953. It is interesting that the ship used to place the new crib was the *Ben Moreel*, which was the former *E. J. Kulas*, renamed after its crash into the original lighthouse.

III. HISTORY OF THE MANY SMALL DOWNRIVER ISLANDS

The early map on page 10 shows all of the islands located on the thirty-two miles of the Detroit River in the mid- to late 1800s. There were twenty-two islands at that time. A close look (see recent chart inside back cover) shows some islands that are no longer visible, and there are some new ones produced since this chart was drawn. The discussion here will center on those islands, both past and current, that are located in the lower portion of the river, namely from Mamajuda south. The order presented will be primarily in the order that they would be seen on the **GUIDED BOAT TOUR** described in the next section. The discussion of each island will include the owner(s), any buildings (current or past), uses over the years, and any other interesting historical information.

GROSSE ILE

Grosse Ile earlier consisted primarily of one large island with several natural canals producing smaller islands within its boundaries. The digging of other canals over the years has produced other small islands. All of these smaller islands, as well as the mainland of Grosse Ile, are discussed in the previous section beginning on page 62.

SLOCUM'S ISLAND (ELIZABETH PARK)

Slocum's Island begins just north of Elizabeth Park in Trenton and continues south of the Detroit Edison Electric Power Plant, consisting of approximately 162 acres. The island includes what is now the Wayne County Park, boat ramp, and marina, as well as the power plant. A detailed discussion of the island is included in the Trenton section, beginning on page 30. This area was originally surrounded by a marsh and was known as "Slocum's Island," after its owner Giles Slocum. The property was given to the county in 1919, under two conditions: the first being that it be renamed Elizabeth Park (in honor of Slocum's granddaughter); and the second, the county had to dredge the marshland around the area to make it an "actual" island. The current canal was dug in 1921 by the Dunbar and Sullivan Company. The marina next to the boat slips was built in 1993.

HUMBUG ISLAND

Humbug Island is south of the Grosse Ile Free Bridge, just off shore from the property owned by McLouth Steel in Gibraltar. It is currently uninhabited with no buildings visible. This was not always the case, as described by this article in the July 7, 1899, *Wyandotte Herald*:

I have often heard of the "Humbug club" and their outing during the summer season. I resolved to visit the scene of the club's annual festivity. Humbug Island is owned by the Slocum family [who owned what is now Elizabeth Park]*, but is inhabited by just one lonely fisherman. An old man named Cahoon passes his life on the island, earning a living by fishing. He enjoys the presence of a visitor, whom he entertains with many reminiscences of early days and big, thumping fish yarns. Sometimes the old man has luck in catching a few sturgeon, which he sells at a good price. Cahoon is an old-*

time fisherman, who has seen good days on the river long before the advent of the big freighters and other ships.

Humbug Island is currently listed as 420 acres belonging to Waste Management Corporation.

CALF ISLAND

Several of the smaller islands located close to Grosse Ile were part of the original Grosse Ile deed given to the Macomb brothers in 1776. Most of these islands, including Calf, were acquired in 1817 by Alexander Macomb, son of one of the original Macomb brothers. During the 1800s, Grosse Ile farmers would take their young livestock to this eleven-acre island to separate them from the others, giving it the name Calf Island.

The eleven-acre island was bought in 1914 by the Marxhausen family. They built a large home there where they entertained many politicians and other influential people. The home was decorated by magnificent carvings and furnished with beautiful antiques. Local folklore has it that most of the valuable antiques were "borrowed" by a local antique dealer in the mid- to late 1950s when vandals began destroying the home. The island was sold in 1974 for a reported $120,000. The house was burned to the ground in the early to mid-1960s. The old home foundation is still visible among the growing underbrush. The island is currently owned by Louis Miller.

SWAN ISLAND

This land was originally known as Snake Island for obvious reasons! It was swampy, unusable property until it was drained and filled. The canal that sepa-rates it from the mainland was dug in the 1920s. It was named after the Swan Family, who were early residents of Grosse Ile.

HORSE ISLAND

Horse Island is part of the city of Gibraltar and was discussed in that section on page 54. It is being mentioned here because many boaters and/or fish-ermen have used this island as a landmark when entering and leaving the river, as well as Lake Erie. It had a pri-vate boat launch ramp, bait shop, and boat rental used by many for years. The original homes were primarily summer cottages, built starting around 1923. The canal on the west side of the island was dug in 1928, and the dredged material was used to backfill the back side of the island, allowing building lots to be sold on both sides of the road. The bait shop and boat rental docks were built in the early 1920s and continued until 1993, when the city bought the property for a potential new bridge.

CELERON (or TAWAS, or TAWAY)

This island got its name from Commandant Pierre Joseph Celeron, a prominent voyageur in the early explorations of the Great Lakes area. The French regarded the island strategic because of its position guarding the entrance to Lake Erie. Celeron frequently garrisoned his army there. He was the son of Captain Jean Baptist Celeron, commander of the first French military force in America.

The island was originally owned by the Potawatomi Indians, as was much of the area. Jean St. Reaume was given the island by the Indians on May 30, 1789. John Askin bought the island for 500 pounds in 1796 and later deeded it to Alexander Macomb in 1817. It later became the property of the John P. Clark family, who in 1889 deeded it to the Lowrie family. The Lowrie family owned the 125-acre island until 1966. During that time they built cottages, a boat house, and a small farm, complete with barns. There was never any electricity, so refrigerators and lights were powered by kerosene, brought across from Horse Island in 55-gallon drums. Heavy items were brought to the island on an Army surplus "duck." They had a well and windmill, but did carry over their own drinking water. The Lowrie family offered the island for sale in the 1961 timeframe. The asking price was $389,000. Taxes at that time were approximately $1,000, payable to Grosse Ile Township and Wayne County.

Celeron Island was purchased from the Lowrie Family by the Celeron Island Corporation in November of 1966. The reported purchase price was $260,000. They had grandiose plans to build a seven to eight-million-dollar complex complete with 300 homes, accessible only by boat, a marina with docking for 200 boats, a boat club, and several recreation areas, including a golf club. The plans also included their own fire and police protection. Dredging and filling actually began for this project in October 1967. Once dredging began, Grosse Ile township sought a restraining order, alleging improper dumping and filling, starting a court battle. This stopped the development.

It became apparent that development plans were not going to materialize for the corporation. The DNR (Department of Natural Resources) bought the island with proceeds received from selling their first series of collector duck stamps.

All of the buildings that once were enjoyed by the Lowrie family and their friends are now gone. There are still some nice beaches along the shoreline that attract some local use. Exploration by foot on the island reveals evidence of old foundations that leave clues to how nice it must have been in earlier days.

SUGAR ISLAND

Sugar Island has enjoyed a rich heritage since its ownership by Alexander Macomb beginning in 1817. It was named for its fine stand of sugar maple trees. It is said to be the site of the largest hardwood tree west of the Alleghenies. The island became the property of John P. Clark during the 1800s, who made substantial improvements. An article in the *Wyandotte Herald*, dated July 15, 1898, describes some of these improvements.

Trustees of the John P. Clark estate are now making improvements at Sugar and Hickory Islands which will make those always delightful spots still more popular with summer resorters. Last spring the dock at Sugar Island was rebuilt and made larger. A kitchen has been built adjoining the east side of the old dancing hall, the latter being transformed into a dining room. E. N. Baisley will have charge of the restaurant and will serve meals regularly seven days a week during the remainder of the excursion season. The restaurant is not open yet, but it is hoped to have it in full blast some time next week. Campers and excursioners can hereafter enjoy all the pleasures of an outing without the discomfort of cooking. Then an elegant new dancing pavilion, measuring 44 × 68 feet, is now nearing completion near the boat landing.

Sugar Island (along with Hickory Island) was a popular destination for the excursion boats from Detroit, Wyandotte, and other areas during the late 1800s. Another article in the *Wyandotte Herald*, dated June 20, 1899, further describes the facilities on the island at that time.

Many improvements have been made at Sugar Island, the popular resort at the mouth of the river. These include a covered waiting room at the dock, the addition of broad verandahs to the Casino, a new building for the hot water boilers, and a fine one-third-mile bicycle track. All the woodwork on the island is bright with new paint, the resort never having been in such fine condition before.

E. N. Baisley, who has charge of the refreshment privilege, is getting everything in apple-pie order at the Casino to accommodate large crowds during the season.

As before, the large, airy dancing pavilion, with its free music, will appeal to many. A well laid out base ball diamond offers attractions to lovers of the national game. Convenience to Hickory Island, where several scores of cottagers spend the heated term, is another advantage.

No better pleasure trip could be conceived than a ride down the beautiful Detroit River on the steamer Wyandotte *to Sugar Island.*

Other publications during the late 1800s and early 1900s reveal the grandeur of Sugar Island during that time. The following are excerpts from brochures published by the Trustees of the Clark Estate in 1900:

Where is the Church or Society to which you belong going for their day's outing? We would advise, before you make up your mind where to go, that you look into the many advantages offered by the managers of Sugar Island.

No liquors of any kind are sold on the island or boat, and this has been much appreciated in the years past by the managers of Church and Sunday School

Wyandotte's Big Day

Board of Commerce Annual Excursion

SUGAR ISLAND

Thursday, June, 14, 1923

Bigger and Better Than Ever!!

The Tashmoo and Greyhound, finest steamers of the White Star Fleet, will carry the crowd.

Free Dancing on the boats and at the island

A splendid program of High School track events. Free for all events.
A base ball game between St. Patrick's and another team in their own league. This is a scheduled league game and will be a hot one.
A dandy bathing beach. A Roller Coaster, Merry-Go-Round and other attractions for the Children. The best Cafeteria to be found in any park or resort around Detroit.
A long list of prizes, including lady's silk fiber sweater, a length of best quality silk dress goods, an exquisite luncheon cloth, case of Heinz products, men's caps, men's shirts, collars, belts and buckles, boxes of cigars, boxes of candy, a dandy coaster wagon for some lucky kid, a Spalding base ball glove, tennis shoes, loving cup and many other articles. Every prize is of first class quality.
There will be novelty stunts both on the boats and at the island.
Every kiddie will be given a souvenir.

IT'S YOUR DAY—COME YOURSELF AND BRING YOUR FAMILY

Fig. 46

Figure 46

Notice from Wyandotte's Board of Commerce, advertising excursions to Sugar Island. It refers to the roller coaster, merry-go-round, cafeteria, track events, and bathing beach which were all present on Sugar Island during that time. (Courtesy of the Wyandotte Historical Society)

Fig. 47

Figure 47

View of Sugar Island in the 1920-30s showing roller coaster and large covered docks. (Courtesy of Burton Historical Collection of the Detroit Public Library)

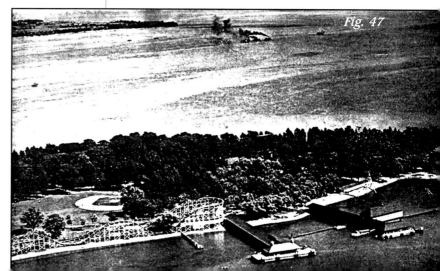

excursions. An abundance of hot water is furnished free for tea and coffee.

Sugar Island is high and dry with shady walks and well-kept lawns and many cozy nooks. If you enjoy a game of base ball our grounds are at your disposal, and no pains or expense have been spared in making them as perfect as possible. You can take your wheel and have a spin on the bicycle path which we have laid out.

For those of you who enjoy dancing, there is a dancing pavilion with hard wood floors which are kept clean and polished. There is an orchestra on the boat and, if you so desire, will stay on the island, playing for the dancing, or if you do not care for the music the orchestra will return on the boat. This is left entirely with the parties giving the excursion.

If a storm comes up there is a long covered dock to protect you from the rain, or the sides of the pavilion can be closed up, making a perfect shelter.

If you enjoy fishing and rowing we have a number of rowboats, safe and commodious, which we will rent at moderate rates by the hour or day. There are many places about Sugar Island where there is bass fishing.

The steamer Wyandotte *which makes the run to Sugar Island was built expressly for this route, and is a speedy, commodious boat, taking you on a trip that is one of the pleasantest and most delightful of the many enjoyable rides you can take from the "City of the Straits."*

We hope that you will give us a share of your patronage and assure you that you will receive full value for your money.

The island remained a popular amusement park attracting thousands during the early 1900s. There were many additions to the island, including a roller coaster and other attractions. The excursion ship *Tashmoo* became one of the primary means of travel to and from the island, stopping there several times a day during the summer months. The grounding of the *Tashmoo*, while going through the Hole-in-the-Wall toward Amherstburg in 1936, began the decline of this once-proud island. The ship apparently hit a loose rock in the narrow passage, while it had nearly 1,400 people on board. She made it to the Canadian shore, where it came to rest on the shallow bottom. All passengers were disembarked safely. The island was abandoned shortly after. Little was done with the island during the late 1930s and 1940s. The buildings and amusement rides fell into disrepair and became the target of vandals. A detailed account of the sinking of the *Tashmoo* is included in the **AMHERSTBURG** section, beginning on page 76.

In 1944, a group of black Detroit businessmen bought the island, citing bans on blacks using other amusement parks in the Detroit area. Facilities were built and boat service to the island started in 1946, but it was never successful.

Dunbar and Sullivan acquired the island in 1952 for payment of accrued taxes. They announced plans to reinstate an old permit that would allow them to build a rock dike in the shallow waters. Their plans included building a dike approximately one mile south of the island, one half mile east, and west to the end of the old amusement park docks. The dike would be filled, but it was not determined with what at this time. These plans drew an outcry from many local groups. Following are excerpts from the *Wyandotte Herald* in 1952, describing some of this outrage:

All-time records for sheer crowd interest and loud protesting will be bro-

on this enlarged Sugar Island ... disputants fear that it would be doomed to die an early death in the lovely waterways north of the Detroit Light.

Historic Sugar Island ... once the terminus of pleasure craft from Detroit ... who brought throngs to enjoy dancing in the beautiful island pavilion or to walk its covered aisles ... has had a hectic career.

Rage for possible loss of scenic beauty, possible blocking of river traffic, and spot for outdoor recreation and sport, residents of Grosse Ile and Hickory Island, and hunters, fishermen and boaters from the area took a stand against the fill.

The plan to fill and develop the island stayed in court for some time. The island structures continued to deteriorate, and in 1954, the great pavilion burned to the ground. The *Wyandotte Herald* wrote this account on August, 19, 1954:

Boatmen-firemen are rare in the Downriver area, and the Sugar Island dance pavilion burned last weekend unattended.

Both Grosse Ile and Trenton fire departments were unable to send equipment to the island, but luck kept the

Figure 48

Another view of Sugar Island showing the grandstand and pavilion, which burned to the ground in 1954. (Courtesy of Burton Historical Collection of the Detroit Public Library)

Figure 49

The dancing pavilion on Sugar Island as it looked around 1910. (Courtesy of Jim Engle)

Figure 50

The steamer Greyhound at one of the docks at Sugar Island. Note the covered dock. Parts of the concrete docks are still in place just off Sugar Island. (Courtesy of Burton Historical Collection of the Detroit Public Library)

ken tomorrow night, when Lt. Col. John D. Bristol holds his hectic hearing about filling around Sugar Island, at Grosse Ile High School.

Spreading of the word through columns of the Tribune's page one last week brought more genuine screams of anguish from Downriver and its sportsmen, fishermen, and riverman than we've had in years.

Battle lines are drawn ... and despite Dunbar & Sullivan's rosy picture of an island paradise, with plenty of small homes and canals for "low income folks"

wind from spreading into the wooded area about the old, large building.

Fig. 51

Cause of the fire was undetermined, but witnesses reported seeing two columns of smoke climbing away from the building.

The island, once a scene of festive gatherings, and recently deserted except for picnics and parties especially planned, is owned by Dunbar and Sullivan Dredging Company.

The company was quoted as saying that its future might include subdivision for homesites. The company acquired the isle just south of Grosse Ile several years ago for the payment of accrued taxes.

The company placed the dancing pavilion's value at $50,000, calling it one of the largest in America.

The original plan for filling submitted in 1952 was later amended after all of the protest. The following article from the *Wyandotte Herald* published on April 23, 1959, describes the more recent proposal:

Sugar Island as an exclusive "Summer Colony" is the plan disclosed this week by Dunbar and Sullivan, owners, if approval is granted by the

U.S. Corps of Engineers on an application for a proposed harbor line.

The 35-acre wooded island which lies 1,000 feet southeast of Grosse Ile (Hickory Island) would provide approximately 250 homesites.

Some summer homesites would be developed around the perimeter of the present Sugar Island, which once was a popular amusement park for Downriver and Toledo residents in the 1920s. The center portion, according to Dunbar and Sullivan, would be reserved for a park and recreation area.

The firm also proposes to fill semi-circle portions of shallow land encircling the east and north. This man-made land would create added summer homesites.

Fig. 52

Contemplated also are picnic and beach areas open to Grosse Ile residents, Sugar Island Yacht Club and a harbor of refuge for boats caught on Lake Erie in storms.

Developers estimate the completed project would hike the assessed value of the land "in excess of $800,000." No figure was placed on the entire project.

Spokesmen for Dunbar and Sullivan said final disposition of the island must

Figure 51

A closeup view of part of the Sugar Island roller coaster with a passenger ship tied up to the docks in the background. (Courtesy of Jim Engle)

Figure 52

A good view of the covered docks at Sugar Island with park visitors in the foreground, circa 1908. (Courtesy of Jim Engle)

be determined in the very near future "or it will be sold." The dredging company acquired the tiny island at the mouth of the Detroit River in a state tax land sale for $15,000 in 1948.

Desire to improve the property and keep company machines and men busy in lull periods plus hopes to eventually develop a small harbor prompted the purchase.

Since that time, fires destroyed all the one-time amusement park buildings and dance hall, and it has been used for Boy Scout, Girl Scout outings, island group picnics who were welcomed, and also by uninvited guests who created disturbances.

After all of the planning and fighting by the various local factions, the Dunbar and Sullivan project to build on the island was turned down by the federal government in August of 1960.

As private boating became more popular in the Downriver area, boaters began to use the island for picnics and overnight camping. It was a favorite spot for many, and most were surprised to see "NO TRESPASSING" signs posted around the island in 1985. It was soon learned that the island had been purchased by a private person, namely Bill Herschler. The article in the *Detroit News* dated May 26, 1985, describes his intention for the island.

His plans for building a home on the uninhabited island are still vague. "First I have to find out about getting electricity, and then I have to get a seawall built," he said.

He's not planning on subdivisions or other developments or any other high-powered business moves. The island, he said, will be his home and no one else's.

At the time of this writing, little has changed on or around the island since the buildings burned and/or deteriorated in the mid-fifties. There is no evidence of the above mentioned dream home, or of the "NO TRESPASSING" signs once located along the beach. Probably, many of the boaters who frequent the island beaches today do not realize they are enjoying someone else's private island.

BOBLO ISLAND (BOIS BLANC)

Complete books could be written about the history of Boblo Island. They may be entitled The Island of "Bois Blanc," however, since that was the original name of the island. This island, the largest of the smaller Downriver islands, is by far the most popular, visited by millions of people from around the world until it was sold to a private investor in 1994. The following article, dated August 12, 1959, in the *Wyandotte Herald* offers a good look at the early history of the island:

It is summer, and like Wyandotte in every summer since 1898, people are boarding the big steamer at Bishop Park to head to Bob-Lo Island.

*It is tradition. It is something for the kids to look forward to, and the parents to remember when the kids yell "Bob-Lo Island!" with exciting cries. The name Bois Blanc is never men-*tioned, even though they are one and the same place.

Bois Blanc is French for "white woods." This derives from the white barked poplar trees which make up much of Bob-Lo Island.

The real name of the island, however, is Etiowiteeddannenti. This is Indian for "a people island of white woods guarding an entrance."

The "people island" refers to the village of Huron Indians on the island, and the "guarding an entrance" is the entry to the Detroit River.

Fig. 53

Figure 53

View of Boblo Island Light after being built in the 1830s. The base still stands on the south end of Boblo.
(Courtesy of Burton Historical Collection of the Detroit Public Library)

Fig. 54

Figure 54

One of the original three blockhouses built by the English on Bois Blanc around 1839. This one still stands on the south end of Boblo Island.
(Courtesy of Burton Historical Collection of the Detroit Public Library)

White men first came to the island in the 1720s when a Jesuit mission was founded there for the Hurons. From this mission, which later left the island, legend says Assumption Catholic Church of Windsor grew.

After the mission, the island became the center of Indian affairs under Mathew Elliott, who built a large homestead there in 1784.

Blanc Island. They were built in 1839, to be used as outposts of Fort Malden. Their military use was short lived, and they became barracks for pensioners until the late 1850s. One was burned to the ground in the 1860s. One still remains on the south end of Boblo.

Other paragraphs from this article refer to who should "own" the island, the United States or the British. The original treaty called for the boundary line between the two countries to be the center of the "navigable" channel separating the countries. At that time, there was only a depth of a few feet on the west side of Bois Blanc, so

Fig. 55

Figure 55

The SS Columbia *built by the Detroit Shipping Company in Wyandotte in 1902. It was 185 feet long, with 2,000 horsepower, and carried approximately 2,500 passengers. (Courtesy of Bill Heinrich)*

When the British had to leave Detroit in 1796, they moved to the head of the Detroit River and erected a military post across from Bois Blanc [what is now Amherstburg]. In time they also put up blockhouses on the [north end of the] island.

Later, after Fort Malden was built in Amherstburg, three larger blockhouses were built toward the south end of Bois

the Americans claimed the only "navigable" channel was between Bois Blanc and what is now Amherstburg (Canada). This would put the boundary in the middle of that channel on the east side of Bois Blanc, making the island American property. Further excerpts from this article include:

How did this misunderstanding [over ownership] turn out? Bois Blanc is

Canadian territory now. During the War of 1812, the island served as a center for the Indian leader, Tecumseh, who organized the Indians against the Americans. America lost the argument.

Following the War, the James Hackett family moved to Bois Blanc as keepers of the lighthouse built there in the 1830s. [The base of the lighthouse still stands on the south end of the island.]

The island came under private ownership in 1869. The Rankin Family bought it for $40 and McKee Rankin and his wife, Kitty Blanchard, both actors, turned it into a gentleman's estate. They entertained "New York's Delmonico crowd and Detroit's Society" lavishly, according to a Detroit newspaper article written during that period . [Other articles refer to their turning one of the original three blockhouses into a headquarters for the estate. They stocked the grounds with deer, wild turkey, and elk, and built extensive house stables.]

It seems Rankin's financial and acting abilities did not coincide. The island was later sold by a mortgage company to two Detroiters.

Modern history began for the island in 1898, when the Detroit Belle Isle and

Fig. 56

Fig. 58

Windsor Ferry Company, encouraged by the success of their excursion business, decided to expand with a run to Bois Blanc.

Figure 56

The SS Ste. Claire was built in 1910 by the Toledo Shipping Company. She was 215 feet long, had 2,000 horse power, and carried approximately 2,500 passengers. (Courtesy of Bill Heinrich)

Figure 58

One of the six smaller Boblo boats that provided service to the island from Gibraltar, Michigan, and Amherstburg, Ontario.

In the beginning, they leased a few acres on the middle of the island, and started to develop it as a pleasure resort. A dock and dance pavilion followed, and on June 18, 1898, the first excursion set out.

Why did the ferry company decide to change the name to Bob-Lo? To tell the truth, it was an effort to keep the Americans from fracturing the French language anymore. Bois Blanc managed to come out sounding like "Boys Blank," so the name was shortened and simplified to Bob-Lo [in 1929], which is closer to the true French pronunciation.

Since 1898, Bois Blanc, or Bob-Lo, by now, has been improved consistently with the addition of dining facilities, baseball fields, boat liveries, bath houses, and of course, rides.

The first "ride" was the father of all amusement park rides, the merry-go-round, which was billed as the "largest in the world" when installed.

In 1913, a dance hall was built, it remains the largest dance hall in Canada, and was also billed as the "largest in the world" when erected.

The above article provides a good description of the early days of Boblo Island. The amusement park continued to grow and eventually consumed 272 acres of the island. Thirty-two rides, such as log water slides, indoor and outdoor roller coasters, bumper cars, and others, along with a large marina for private boaters, were added over the years. It became one of the most popular destinations for Detroit area residences, as well as visitors from around the world, especially close-by states and Canada.

Annual attendance would approach one million into the 1980s, and over 800 people found summer jobs operating and maintaining the park.

The following article from the *Detroit Free Press* on March 9, 1994, describes memories of the island during it heydays:

For people who have been there over and over or even just once, Boblo Island holds vivid memories—a first kiss on the boat on the way to the island, the romance of the ride home late at night, Captain Boblo in his official hat waving good-bye to boats departing from the dock.

On Tuesday, many Detroiters were shocked to hear that the island will be sold off. Here are some favorite memories.

Joanna Gunn, 80, who now lives in Charlevoix, says her earliest memories were of church picnics at the island in the early 1920s.

"The picnics were always in June, and the picnickers would gather at the foot of Woodward, their baskets filled with potato salad and baked beans, to take on the boats. Girls wore dresses and bloomers.

"The island was a big park, kind of like a city park," Gunn says. "There were only a handful of rides then, including bumper cars that ran around and bumped into each other."

After a day at the park, the group would have a late supper at the end of the day, made up of picnic leftovers, and take the late boat home. At the end of the day, they'd wind up at Vernor's for a glass of ginger ale.

Florence Karrer of St. Clair Shores remembers Boblo as a hot spot for young men and women in the early 1930s. She still has a scrapbook that shows a picture of her junior class at Annunciation High School in a 1931 excursion to Boblo. The eleven people in the photograph are all well-dressed, the girls wearing hats and the men in dressy white flannel pants and dark coats. "To us, it was a very special occasion, and we dressed that way—Boblo was really the place to go."

Karrer took her own children to Boblo in the 1950s and a few years ago, her grandchildren.

Former Mayor Coleman Young was denied entrance to Boblo in 1931, when he was a student at St. Mary's Catholic School in Detroit. In his autobiography, he wrote about how that event marked his life.

For Ann Hunt, 79, her fondest memories of Boblo are dancing. "The park had the most wonderful dance floor on earth. It was divine, polished. It was just beautiful, big and airy. There were live orchestras and moonlight cruises. If you got lucky and some fellow asked you to go, you'd have dinner on the boat or at the island, and come back in the dark."

Her family made trips every year to Boblo when she was a child. Whenever visitors came to town, one highlight was always Boblo.

Geraldine Neill-McLaughlin, 32, of Amherstburg, Ontario, is the daughter of Eric Neill, a former owner of Boblo. She visited Boblo regularly as a child, and started working there at 17.

"I went on all the moonlight cruises, and heard people like Tommy Dorsey play. That was one of the perks of being the owner's daughter."

Ted Diesbourg held nearly every job there was at Boblo. He recalls that various owners in the past two decades sometimes tended to make decisions on impulse. About ten years ago, for example, management decided to create a new roller coaster ride, the corkscrew, from parts of other rides.

"It came up four feet short, and we had to order the four feet of track from Europe, but it was ready in time."

Boblo Island meant a day of rides, dancing, and a river trip to Tom Keiswetter, 48. He says: "I remember the excitement and anticipation of getting to this place. It was our Disney World."

Boblo amusement park's popularity increased from its start in 1898, into the 1980s, attracting nearly one million visitors a year. Its long dive in popularity began in the early 1980s, when bankruptcy forced an electrical shutdown of the island for two days. Automobile Club of America (AAA) acquired the island in 1983 from the Boblo Island Amusement Company for a reported $6.5 million and spent $14 million in renovations, only to sell it to the International Broadcasting Corporation in 1988, for a reported $20 million. IBC then filed for Chapter 11 reorganization three years later.

Some of the reasons for the demise of the island's popularity are discussed in the following article in the *News Herald,* dated March 13, 1994:

Boblo is a metropolitan Detroit landmark despite the fact that it lies in Canadian waters, Yet, after five different owners in the past 15 years, it appears that time, more than anything else, has passed Boblo by.

Boblo's appeal as an amusement park lay in more simple times. Times when Detroit was the hub of the area's activity and people headed downtown with regularity. Times when the hour's journey to Boblo on one of its old paddlewheelers was truly appreciated. Times when places like Cedar Point, King's Island, and Disney World didn't even exist.

Detroit's high crime rate and general deterioration kept people away from the Boblo docks. The long boat rides became an irritation instead of a lure in the fast-paced 1990s. Boblo's popularity as an amusement park was far overshadowed by the constant modernization of rides at other, more resort type parks.

The primary means of transportation to and from Boblo was provided by two large steamers, the SS *Columbia* and the SS *Ste. Claire*. The *Columbia* was built in 1902 by the Detroit Shipbuilding Company of Wyandotte. It was 185 feet long, with 2,000 horsepower. The *Ste. Claire* was built in 1910 by the Toledo Shipbuilding Company. She was 215 feet in length and also had 2,000 horsepower. Both steamers could carry approximately 2,500 passengers. Their primary port-of-call was Detroit, but over the years they also departed from Wyandotte, and possibly other Downriver communities. Many moonlight cruises included live bands and dancing, and other special memories were created by several marriages and receptions taking place on the boats. The boat ride from Detroit to Boblo is thirty-six miles round trip and took over an hour each way. To many visitors over the years, the boat ride was half of the fun of going to Boblo. This continued until 1991, when both of these large steamers were sold. The buyer of both boats failed to make payments, so they became the property of the Detroit Economic Growth Corporation in 1993 and continued to be moored along the Detroit River at Ecorse. They came up for federal auction early in 1996, when several communities, including Riverview, were considering bidding. It ended up that a private foundation bought both boats for a $1 bid in a controversial auction. The foundation's announced plans call for selling one boat and converting the other to a cruising nautical museum. The other private investor interested in buying the boats claimed he would have paid considerably more than the $1, and he had planned on restoring both boats to operate cruises along the Detroit River.

To supplement travel to Boblo from Detroit, ferry service was established from Amherstburg, Ontario, and from Gibraltar. The Gibraltar ferries began service in 1984. Following the sale of the large steamers in 1991, these six remaining small ferryboats were the primary means of transportation to and from Boblo. These boats ranged from 60 feet, carrying 250 passengers, to 94 feet, carrying 550 passengers. There was also a marina on the west side of the island with room for over 100 private boaters to use while visiting the island.

The last owners who tried to keep the island alive as an amusement park bought the island at an auction sale from bankrupt IBC in 1993 for $3.7 million. The group was from the Seattle, Washington, area and was represented by Michael Moodenbaugh. He was a very dynamic person who had big ideas for renovating the park. His plans included new rides, concerts, an improved marina, etc. He nearly doubled the park's attendance from about 200,000 visitors in 1992, to nearly 400,000 in 1993.

Along with his successes in his first year, he also had several public relations incidents that drew unfavorable press. These included cutting off the water supply to a 72-year-old-widow, whose family had owned a cottage on the island for years. When articles concerning this incident hit the local newspapers, fishermen and other boaters began dropping off five-gallon jugs of water on the widow's dock.

He also had some trouble with the Canadian Coast Guard regarding operation of the ferries running out of Canada. The other incident that resulted in some adverse press surrounded his reported stringent rules for the young park employees. There was labor unrest, apparently caused by possible firings for not picking up scrap paper or other litter.

Nonetheless, Moodenbaugh appeared to be making the amusement park successful again, until he was involved in a nearly fatal automobile accident in the fall of 1993. Since he was practically a "one man show" as far as managing the island was concerned, the anticipation of him being incapacitated for a long time

prompted his financial backers to want out of the Boblo Island amusement park business. Thus, the island was again for sale! With Moodenbaugh in the hospital, Northern Capital (Seattle group) assumed managing control of Boblo and began actions leading to the announcement that the park's rides, and perhaps the island itself, would be sold.

The following article in the *Detroit Free Press*, dated August 10, 1994, describes the most recent sale of Boblo:

John Oram says it all started around April 12 [1994] *when he wondered out loud to Essex-Windsor Member of Parliament Susan Whelan, whether he could buy one of the old Boblo Island Amusement park rides for his kids.*

"She said well, you know, the whole island is for sale," he recalled. And I said,"I can't buy Boblo Island!...Come on. I just want a little ride!"

Four months later, Oram bought Boblo Island.

The following excerpts from the *News Herald*, dated July 31, 1996, reveal Boblo's transformation from a once famous amusement park to a first-class residential community:

"This is little Mackinac, Traverse Bay, Martha's Vineyard. This is your big yacht. This is your year-round summer home."

That's the vision of John Oram, the present owner of Boblo Island.

After a half hour on the island, it is evident that Oram's dreams of Bois Blanc Island Community are not what many naysayers have described as pie in the sky, but are well-thought-out ideas rapidly taking shape.

The ferry is in place, the marina is open. One home is nearly completed and eight other homes have begun construction. Infrastructure and roads are in place for the first phase of 52 homes on the north end and 28 of those lots have been sold (six to Michigan Downriver residents).

Oram pledged that the island will be fully developed in three years.

One fact that's little known to the general public is that there is a nine-hole golf course in the center of the northern end of the island. The course hasn't been used in decades and is wildly overgrown. Within the next year, however, it will be restored.

The course will provide the back-drop for about half the homes of the first phase, all of which are marketed as either river or golf course homes.

While none of the homes will have their own boat dock, Oram said the landowners will have first choice to reserve a boat slip [in the Boblo marina].

Oram said only residents will be allowed to bring cars onto the island. Visitors will be ferried over separately. There are two 24-hour auto ferries that ply the 1,000 foot distance between the island and Amherstburg every five minutes. One ferry can carry six cars, the other twelve.

Prior to the sale of the island to Oram, Northern Capital had sold off most of the amusement park rides for a reported $2 million. This plus the proceeds from the sale still left them short of their investments, leaving 270 unsecured creditors.

LIVINGSTONE CHANNEL

The Livingstone Channel today appears to be located along many long finger-shaped islands at the lower end of the Detroit River. Originally there were no long islands in the area, and the only part of the river deep enough to be navigable was the channel between Bois Blanc Island and the mainland of Canada, now known as the Amherstburg Channel. All ship traffic passing through the Detroit River had to pass through this channel. The area of the current Livingstone Channel was originally a shallow (three to four feet) portion of the river with a limestone bottom.

The chart in Figure 59 shows the south end of the Detroit River during the mid-1870s, before the Livingstone Channel project was begun. The Lime Kiln Crossing area, which is north of Bois Blanc, had been dredged by the Americans beginning in 1876, to allow a deep channel all the way to Lake Erie. Prior to dredging, the Lime Kiln Crossing was only about twelve feet deep, which limited the shipping travel. Since approximately 80% of the ship traffic in those days was American tonnage, the U.S. Congress authorized the funds necessary to begin this project. Drilling into the limestone rock was done by hand through three-inch-diameter pipes to a depth of approximately four feet. Explosives were placed into the drilled holes and detonated to break the rock up, allowing it to be scooped up, and stacked off to the side, forming part of what is now known as Crystal Bay. Also note on this chart the shape of Stony Island and the railroad bridge leading to it.

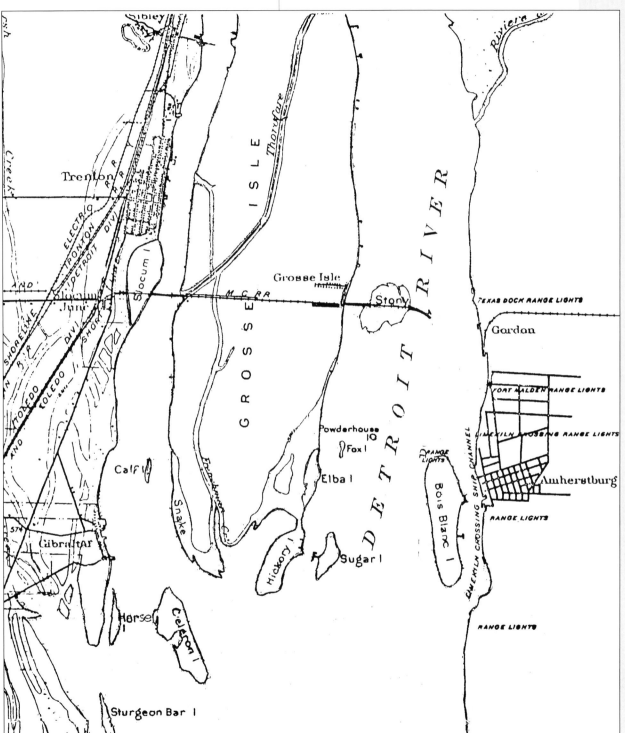

Figure 59

Chart shows the south end of the Detroit River as it looked in the mid-1870s. Construction of the Livingstone Channel did not begin until 1907.

Figure 60

The north end of the Livingstone Channel was dug from 1907 through 1912. The area was drained to allow it to be deepened. This shows workmen with a temporary bridge in the background. (Courtesy of the Grosse Ile Historical Society)

Shipping of freight and passengers continued to grow in the Great Lakes around the turn of the century and into the 1900s. This was especially true of traffic using the Detroit River. The single channel between Bois Blanc and Canada was becoming a bottleneck. Many people had proposed constructing a second channel. The following excerpt from the Annual Report of the Lake Carrier's Association publication in 1907, describes the situation during that time:

In 1906, the Lake Carrier's Association called attention to the great and rapidly growing necessity for a second channel in the Lime Kiln Crossing area [current Livingstone Channel area]. Estimated cost was $6,600,000. Records showed 25,000 vessels crossed this area during [the] 1906 season. One ship every 13 minutes with an average load of 2,800 tons. Also fourteen regular first class passenger steamers crossing that point. Also a "mosquito" fleet—small boats—that cause annoyance. A sinking of any modern ship would completely block the entire movement of tonnage [and passengers] to and from Lake Erie.

During 1906, 7,500,000 passengers traveled the Detroit River, which is 1,500,000 more than all other districts on the Great Lakes combined. Almost 50 groundings were recorded in this area during 1906.

The Federal Government established The River and Harbor Act on March 2, 1907, which appropriated $6,670,950 for the construction of a second channel in the lower Detroit River. This was to be the largest and most expensive project of this type ever attempted in the United States. It included damming off the areas to be dredged and doing the excavation in the dry. This project is what produced the many compensat-

Figure 61

Since the Livingstone Channel was "dry," the workmen could utilize land vehicles during the digging project. (Courtesy of the Grosse Ile Historical Society)

ing dikes and cofferdams close to Stony Island, which to the layman look and act like the finger islands surrounding the Livingstone Channel.

As mentioned, prior to this great project, there had been dredging along the original channel just upbound from Bois Blanc (also known as Ballard's Reef Channel). The Livingstone Channel project was to begin at the Ballard's Reef Channel and travel into the deep water of Lake Erie, past Stony and Bois Blanc islands, for approximately twelve

miles. The first six miles would be cut through limestone.

Actual construction of the channel began on July 20, 1907. It was completed approximately five years later, and it officially opened on October 19, 1912, at a reported cost of approximately $7,000,000. It was named for William Livingstone. Headquarters for the operation were located on Stony Island. See the section on **Stony Island** for more details of how that island was developed during this period.

This original Livingstone project deposited the stone and dredging materi-

al forming the cofferdams and dikes making up the north end of what is seen as the Livingstone Channel. This produced what eventually would become the west side of the popular Crystal Bay anchorage area. The southern end of the original channel was deepened in the mid-1950s, forming the long finger-like dikes now visible south of the Hole-in-the-Wall. Other dredging projects during the same period of time produced the cofferdam

extending from the south end of Boblo Island, which would become known as

Figure 62

The workmen utilized explosives, steam, and muscle power during the six-year project. Their headquarters were on Stony Island, where there was a school, store, and over thirty houses. (Courtesy of the Grosse Ile Historical Society)

Figure 63

Another picture of the heavy steam equipment used while digging the Livingstone Channel. (Courtesy of the Grosse Ile Historical Society)

Figure 64

A good view of what the bottom of the river looked like while the Livingstone Channel was being dug. (Courtesy of the Grosse Ile Historical Society)

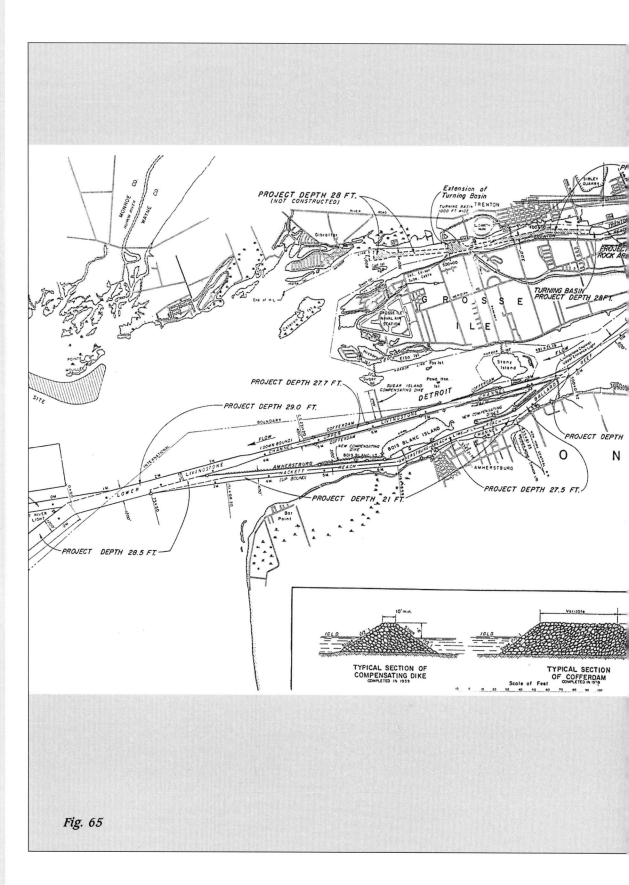

Figure 65

Chart showing the lower end of the Detroit River after completion of Living-stone Channel projects.

Fig. 65

White Sands. The east side of Crystal Bay was also produced during the mid-1950s, by dredging taking place along the Amherstburg Channel. There were several dredging projects during that time that resulted in "Hidden Lake" beside Crystal Bay and the "Horseshoe" anchorage area just north of Boblo Island. The chart in Figure 65 shows the lower end of the Detroit River as it looks since the Livingstone Channel projects were completed.

POWDER HOUSE ISLAND

Powder House Island (sometimes called Dynamite Island) is a small island located just west of the Hole-in-the-Wall in the Livingstone Channel. Local folklore says it got its name from being the storage spot for the explosives used during construction of the Livingstone Channel. However, careful review of nautical charts of the area prior to 1900 show that Powder House Island was already there and named, before the Livingstone Channel was ever started. There were dredging projects north of Amherstburg prior to that time that may have used the island for storage, possibly giving it its name. It is currently privately owned.

Fig. 66

FOX ISLAND

Fox Island is located between Powder House Island and Elba Island (part of Grosse Ile). There once was a private summer cottage owned by the Dominic Gorno family on the island. They used it for family and social gatherings of up to seventy or eighty people nearly every Sunday in the mid-1970s. Vandals got the best of the building prior to its burning down. It is currently owned by the Bob Brown family.

STONY ISLAND

From 1873 to 1888, trains running between Chicago and Buffalo crossed from Grosse Ile to Stony Island by bridge

Fig. 67

Figure 66

The railroad bridge between Grosse Ile and Stony Island was built in 1872. It carried the Michigan Central Railroad cars to Stony Island, where they were loaded on a ferry to reach Canada. The service lasted until 1888. The bridge was removed following the construction of the Livingstone Channel in 1913. (Courtesy of the Grosse Ile Historical Society)

Figure 67

Picture of students in front of the Stony Island Schoolhouse circa 1908. There was a community of approximately thirty homes on the island during the construction of the Livingstone Channel. (Courtesy of the Grosse Ile Historical Society)

Figure 68

One of the buildings on Stony Island used during the construction of the Livingstone Channel. The river was pumped dry, so railroad tracks could be used to move heavy machinery around. (Courtesy of the Grosse Ile Historical Society)

and then onto the Canadian shore by ferry. Stony Island was the center of activity during the construction of the Livingstone Channel from 1907 to 1912.

A general store that offered some postal service, a combination school-church-dance-assembly hall, and some thirty houses were all located on the island during this time. Many of the houses were moved to Grosse Ile after the Livingstone project was completed. The

Figure 69

Another view of the buildings and activity on Stony Island during the Livingstone Channel construction days. (Courtesy of the Grosse Ile Historical Society)

bridge between Stony Island and Grosse Ile was removed in 1913. Stony Island has been for sale for many years. At one time, local investors were interested in the island, hoping to develop it with

upscale homes. The project would have included building a new bridge to Grosse Ile where the old railroad bridge had been.

MAMAJUDA ISLAND

Only relatively long-time Downriver boaters will remember seeing Mamajuda Island. It was located between Fighting Island and the north end of Grosse Ile. It was an important landmark for early river travelers, as it had a lighthouse and small farm. The following article from the *Detroit News* dated September 10, 1969, gives a good historical account of the since disappeared island:

Though a landmark for as long as ships have sailed the river, Mamajuda is hardly more than a large, brush-covered rock outcropping between Fighting Island's lower end and the upper end of Grosse Ile. Officially consisting of 29 or 30 acres, it is much less, particularly at high water.

Silas Farmer's history in 1880 spelled the name MamaJuda and said it was named for an Indian squaw who, before 1807, camped on the island annually for fishing and eventually died there.

Burton's history called her Mammy Judy, and many seamen refer to the island that way. Some historians assume that "Judy" or "Juda" is a corruption of a French or Indian name.

For decades, Mamajuda had a resident lightkeeper. A simple black skeleton tower supporting an automatic flashing white light long since took the place of the lighthouse.

Though tiny, the island is significant to mariners because it is near a junction of channels and a distant turn in the main ship channel, and it marks the edge of a long stretch of shoal water

Fig. 70

between it and Wyandotte.

The original lighthouse was thirty-four feet high and was built in 1849. It was rebuilt in 1866 and burned a steady red light.

A baby girl (Dorothy) was born in 1901 to the third of five lighthouse keepers to tend the light. She never left the island until starting school at age eight. Her lightkeeper father, James Story, rowed her a mile to school each summer school day in Wyandotte, and picked her up the same way. The family rented an apartment on the mainland during the winter until the ice broke up, signaling a new shipping season. She graduated from Grosse Ile High School. Her family eventually was transferred to another local lighthouse. She was married and remained in the

Downriver area till her death in 1989.

The War Department of the United States Government made an application to the Port of Detroit Commission in 1940 to connect the islands of Mamajuda, Mud, and Grassy with fill. This would have produced a large island of approximately 680 acres. The proposal was opposed by most Downriver communities, businesses, and Lake Carriers Association. The main criticism for this was that there was no definite plan for the area when completed, and it might be a hindrance to river navigation. The nearly unanimous opposition killed the project.

High water in the 1950s finally took its toll on the buildings and lighthouse foundation located on Mamajuda. By the early 1960s, there was only a large boulder and shattered tree marking the sandy shoal that was once an inhabited island. The city of Wyandotte had been trying to annex both Mamajuda and Grassy Island for some time. An act of the U.S. Congress dated August 3, 1961, officially deeded these two islands to Wyandotte for use as a National Wildlife Refuge. Grassy Island is now owned by

Fig. 71

Figure 70

Old picture of Mamajuda Island when it consisted of nearly thirty acres. There was a lighthouse, complete with keepers quarters and small farm, until high water began taking its toll in the 1950s. It was located between the north end of Grosse Ile and Fighting Island. (Courtesy of the Wyandotte Historical Society)

Figure 71

The original Mamajuda Lighthouse was built in 1849. It was replaced by the pictured lighthouse in 1866, where it was occupied for decades. One particular family lived there from about 1899 to 1910. The lighthouse keeper's daughter had to be rowed back and forth to school in Wyandotte each summer school day. (the Ile Camera)

the U.S. Fish and Wildlife Service.

IV. A GUIDED HISTORICAL BOAT TOUR ON THE RIVER

This section of **OUR "DOWNRIVER" RIVER** includes a description of many things and places located in the lower Downriver area that have nautical historical value. It is designed as a historical guided tour of the area that could be taken by boat. The tour will begin at the north end of Wyandotte, head south down the Trenton Channel to the beginning of Lake Erie, circle the many islands near the mouth of the river, pass through the south end of the Livingstone Channel, go back up the Amherstburg Channel on the east side of Boblo Island past Crystal Bay, cross back to the east side of Grosse Ile, and end up at Hennepin Point on the north end of Grosse Ile. The points of interest will be numbered starting with #1 and continuing through #63 in roughly the same order they will be visible on the tour. The description of points of interest will be brief in some instances and longer on others, depending on the subject. Some of the items (such as bridges to Grosse Ile!) have been described in some detail in a previous chapter; the page number referring to the page where it was discussed in the main text will be included on such items. Follow the chart located inside the back cover and enjoy the tour.

C A U T I O N :

If you plan on taking a boat on the tour, make sure to check the nautical charts before leaving. Some areas, especially the east side of Grosse Ile and around Celeron Island, contain shallow and dangerous areas. A good understanding of nautical charts and local knowledge is necessary for a safe trip.

As you begin your tour on what is currently called the Trenton Channel, you will be navigating on what was once called "The Great All-American Channel." This channel begins at the north end of Grosse Ile and extends 1,700 feet past the Free Bridge. The following excerpts from an article in the August 28, 1939, *Wyandotte Herald* pretty well describes the magnitude of the project at that time:

NINE DREDGING BOATS RUSH TO COMPLETE [the] GREAT ALL-AMERICAN CHANNEL FOR OCEAN VESSEL TRAFFIC. COMPANIES TO BUILD UNLOADING WHARVES

Tremendous vistas of industrial and commercial development of the Detroit Riverfront from Ecorse through to Lake Erie are being opened by the completion of The All-American Channel, which is to be finished about July 1, 1940, according to the head of operations for the Dunbar and Sullivan Dredging Company. Some 125 men and eight specialized craft are rushing the channel work.

Large companies, including coal and coke ovens, freight terminals, power plants, steel mills, and other manufacturing operations, have promised to build tremendous wharves extending into the river to allow these vessels from all over the world to discharge their cargo economically and efficiently.

The Trenton Channel will be one of the greatest man-made deepwater channels anywhere in the world in fresh water; in making the tremendous cut under the waters of the rushing Detroit River, the dredging operation must remove some 273,000 yards of rock and 322,000 yards of mud, or "overburden," as the engineers say. This blasting of rock which can be heard by residents of the Downriver area is made possible by the geological formation of the Niagara limestone. Very light charges of powder are used.

In the little better than three miles of the channel, which extends 100 feet below the Toll Bridge to 1,500 feet below the County Free Bridge, there will be one tremendous turning basin for boats to maneuver about and change directions if necessary. This basin, which will be located in front of the Trenton Edison plant, will be 1,000 feet long by 1,200 feet wide.

Cost of the deepening operations, which was estimated by the government at $1,243,619, is to be completed by the Dunbar and Sullivan Company for $868,262. This company is the oldest firm on the Great Lakes, having been in the business for over 100 years.

There were proposals on the American side since the turn of the century to improve the Trenton Channel for a shipping lane. The U.S. Government spent over $2 million deepening the Amherstburg Channel (in Canadian territory) in 1903 (just east of current Crystal Bay) to provide one good shipping route from Detroit into Lake Erie. Many American citizens, especially in the Downriver area, were upset with money being spent in another country. Shortly after the Amherstburg Channel was improved, it became general knowledge that a second channel was needed for the increased shipping and for safety. Once again, the Downriver communities lobbied heavily to have this second channel dug along the American shoreline. They lost again, as the decision was made to build the Livingstone Channel, which was started in 1907 (discussed starting on page 104).

When the proposal was again presented to have the Trenton Channel deepened (in the mid-1930s), it was referred to as "The All American Channel," since it would be located all within American waters. As your depth meter will tell you as you travel south along the Trenton Channel, the project was completed to just past the Trenton Edison Electric Plant. The many wharves hoped for along the way never came to be. In fact, much of the industry that the project was designed to help is no longer located along the river. There were those that proposed the channel be extended all the way to Lake Erie, to further enhance American shipping. This proposal had been in the planning stages for over twenty-five years, when it was killed in 1975 by the U.S. Army Corps of Engineers.

Figure 72

Doyle's hoop and stave mill located at the current site of the Wyandotte Hospital. It operated from 1885 to 1902 and employed over 125 people. (Courtesy of the Wyandotte Historical Society)

Now back to your nautical history tour:

#01 - PREVIOUS LOCATION OF MICHIGAN ALKALI COMPANY

(page 16) This company was part of the massive chemical industry beginning in Wyandotte in 1890. This was the location of the North Plant, built in 1895. It became Wyandotte Chemicals in 1943 and was sold to Badische Aniline and Soda Fabrik (BASF) in 1970.

#02 - PREVIOUS LOCATION OF WYANDOTTE BOAT COMPANY

There were several shipbuilding companies located along the river in Wyandotte from the early 1870s until 1920. This was one of the largest. Over 200 ships were built and launched during that time in Wyandotte for commercial use on the Great Lakes

#03 - PREVIOUS LOCATION OF D. H. BURRELL AND COMPANY HOOP AND STAVE WORKS

This factory was built in 1885, at the location of the current Wyandotte Hospital. Logs were floated down the river from Canada and stored in a bay (current location of WYC) and later used to make cheese boxes, hoops, and staves for barrels and kegs. Over 125 people were employed. The factory closed in 1902.

#04 - WYANDOTTE YACHT CLUB (WYC)

was formed in 1952. The clubhouse is on land leased from the Wyandotte Boat Club (WBC). They have approximately 250 members and dockage for 80 boats.

#05 - WYANDOTTE BOAT CLUB (WBC)

is located behind WYC. It was organized in 1875. The first clubhouse, which burned in 1903, was located on the river at the foot of Vinewood. The Wyandotte American Legion clubhouse became headquarters in 1923. The current clubhouse was built in 1946 on land donated to them by Wyandotte Chemical in 1944. The WBC has had many successful teams and individuals, and it won National Championships in 1892, 1928, and 1943. They will be moving their activity to a new facility near a park under construction on the river on the south end of Wyandotte (#10 on tour).

#06 - PREVIOUS LOCATION OF EUREKA BREWING AND ICE COMPANY.

One of several breweries located in Wyandotte at the turn of the century.

#07 - PREVIOUS LOCATION OF MARKS BROTHERS BREWERY.

Location of another early Wyandotte brewery.

#08 - PREVIOUS LOCATION OF EUREKA IRON COMPANY

(page 13), which was built in 1855, on a parcel of land containing 2,000 acres, with nearly two miles of riverfront. The name was changed to Eureka Iron and Steel Company in 1864, when they also began to manufacture steel. The factory became nationally famous for running the first Bessemer process in the United

States in 1865, and for manufacturing the first steel rails and iron railroad ties. It furnished employment for the majority of Wyandotte citizens from 1855 to 1890.

#09 - PREVIOUS LOCATION OF DETROIT DOCK COMPANY

where the first iron hulled-ship was built in Wyandotte in 1872. It was taken over in 1899 by the American Shipbuilding Company, where they used it primarily for steel-hull construction. After launching the hull in Wyandotte, it would be towed to their Detroit plant, where the boilers and other machinery and upper works would be installed. The boatyard closed in 1922.

#10 - PREVIOUS LOCATION OF MICHIGAN ALKALI, SOUTH PLANT

(page 15), this is the location of the first chemical plant in Wyandotte. It was built in 1891, on sixty-one riverfront acres by J. B. Ford (and Company). It was originally built for the purpose of making soda ash needed for plate glass manufacturing. After becoming **Michigan Alkali** in 1895, it became the headquarters for heavy chemical production, including lime kilns, chlorine liquefaction, cement production, lye plant, plating shop, etc. Much of Hennepin Point (Item #63 on tour) was produced by filling marshland with waste from production at these plants. A dry ice plant was one of the last operations added to the south plant in 1932. It eventually became the world's largest dry ice manufacturing facility and operated until 1963. The dry ice plant was demolished in 1972. The land was developed into a nine-hole par-three golf course and home to the Wyandotte Boat Club beginning in 1994

(opened 1996). The land was considered "unbuildable-but-not-unusable," and became a national model for other developers trying to reclaim land polluted by heavy industry. Part of the reclaiming process required that the whole parcel be covered by at least three feet of clean fill dirt to bury any contaminant. This required approximately 500,000 cubic yards of fill to be hauled in, ending up with a rolling terrain that is three to twenty feet above the original level.

#11 - GROSSE ILE TOLL BRIDGE

(page 67) was completed in 1913 by E. W. Voigt. He owned most of the north end of Grosse Ile, where he raised horses. He also owned a brewery in Detroit. Local folklore has it that he built the bridge primarily to get his horses back and forth to the brewery to pull the wagons. There has been controversy surrounding the bridge practically from when it was built up to the late 1940s, including the county trying to buy it, court battles over fares, etc. It has been hit by freighters on two occasions, once in 1965 and again in 1992. Luckily there were no deaths or injuries either time. The bridge was last offered for sale in 1981, but there were no takers. It is still privately owned.

#12 - PREVIOUS LOCATION OF WATERMAN FERRY DOCK AND HOME OF C. D. WATERMAN

(page 73). This was the location of one of the early ferry services, providing service between Grosse Ile and Trenton in the 1860-70s. Horses, wagons, farm machinery, and later automobiles were transported to the mainland by a scow towed by a launch. The property was owned by the wealthy C. D. Waterman, who financed the first telephone cable to

Figure 73

Harry Bennett's boathouse, built in 1939, by Henry Ford's controversial personnel director for a reported $1.5 million. This pagoda-shaped house has a small house across the street connected by a tunnel to the main house.

cross over to Grosse Ile in 1890. His son invented the nation's first outboard motor and tested it, in 1905, along the channel in this area.

#13 - PREVIOUS LOCATION OF THE DETROIT BOAT WORKS

A. J. Liggett and Son Company expanded its boatbuilding facilities in 1917 to the foot of Sibley Road. They built 30- to 35-foot quality mahogany cruisers with a workforce ranging from 50 to 250. During World War II, they turned to the production of 110-foot sub-chasers. The tenth and last sub-chaser was built in 1943. After that, they discontinued building boats, and moved their business to the foot of Walnut (#19 on tour), where they sold Chris Craft boats.

#14 - HARRY BENNETT'S BOATHOUSE

Harry Bennett was Henry Ford's right-hand man and Ford Motor Company's personnel director. He was known as a heavy-handed character who could handle himself in tough situations. He built this pagoda-shaped house in 1939 at a reported cost of $1.5 million. The lower section on the river side is a boathouse with room for several good-sized cruisers. There is a tunnel between the main house and a

smaller house on the east side of the road. There are three entrances to the tunnel, two of which are concealed. A tool cabinet in the boat well slides out of the way when triggered, and the wall of a bedroom closet moves aside when triggered. It has been for sale and sold several times over the years.

Fig. 73

15 - McLOUTH STEEL TRENTON PLANT.

This plant was built on its 210-acre parcel in 1948. The ore docks were built as part of a major expansion program in 1953.

Figure 74

View of McLouth's Trenton Plant as it looked after being built in 1948. The big ore dock, as well as other improvements, were not added until 1953.
(Detroit Times, November 1, 1953)

Fig. 74

The plant has had financial problems since the early 1980s. It was purchased by the employees in 1988, but still continued to struggle. It was announced in March of 1996 that it would be shut down until further notice.

#16 - ORIGINAL LOCATION OF PURDY BOAT WORKS

(page 42). Neal Purdy opened his boat works where they built big, beautiful yachts up to 72 feet long, just south of the current hospital location in 1917. They also built Bimini Babies, which were 18-foot racing boats capable of 40+ mph and sold for $2,800. The boat works was moved to the foot of Walnut (#19 on tour) in 1920, where it remained in operation until 1925. The building became vacant after that.

#17 - ANDERSON HOUSE

is one of the few "boathouses" that survived along the waterfront over the years. Early in the 1900s, the shoreline of Grosse Ile and Trenton were lined with these houses, which were used primarily as cottages during the summer. High water and ice led to the demise of most of these old buildings over the years. This boathouse was originally built in the 1915 era as a summer cottage for an owner who was planning to cut black walnut timber off the island to be sold for gun stocks. The end of World War I reduced the need for gun stocks, so his walnut

timber venture was short-lived. In fact, the current owner found many walnut planks that had been used for construction in building the house. The house was used as a "sail repair" facility and later as a drop-off point during the rumrunning days. There was still a trap door leading into the lower basement (boat storage area) when the current owner acquired the house in 1982.

#18 - WEST SHORE GOLF AND COUNTRY CLUB

was founded in 1908. The original clubhouse was an attractive home built in the 1870s.

Fig. 75

Fig. 76

Figure 75

The Anderson (current owners) home is one of the few "boathouses" that survived high water, ice, and neglect over the years. This home was built around 1915 and was used for many purposes over the years, including sail repair and as a drop off point in the rumrunning days.

Figure 76

The Grosse Ile (as well a Trenton, Wyandotte, etc.) shoreline was lined with "boathouses" in the early 1900s. This is a typical view of the river bank in 1909.
(Courtesy of Jim Engle)

#19 - FERRY ROAD
led to a dock on the channel that served the first ferry boats between Grosse Ile and Trenton in the 1860-70s.

#20 - PREVIOUS LOCATION OF TURNER BOATYARD
(page 35). The oldest boatyard in Trenton began building ships in the late 1860s. They built at least thirty-six ships, eighteen of which were steamships. As many as 350 men were employed at one time during the eight years of operation. There were sometimes as many as five ships being built at one time. Several other boatbuilding companies took over this location throughout the years, including Purdy Boat Works, Davis Boat Yard, and Liggett's Chris Craft Sales. The Liggett building was torn down in 1968. A "Liggett and Son Boat Works" painted wooden sign was still located, though barely readable, on Riverside Drive at the foot of Walnut, until torn away during filling operations in 1994.

#21 - MOBIL OIL DOCK.
This dock was for tankers delivering petroleum to the refinery that was located at the corner of West and Allen roads. There were originally three pipelines running from this dock to the refinery site. The refinery was torn down in 1994.

#22 - SLOCUM'S ISLAND
(page 89) was owned by the Slocum family. It was given to Wayne County as their first park unit in 1919, as a generous gift, with two conditions. The first condition was that its name be changed to Elizabeth Park, after the granddaughter of the original owner. The second was that Wayne County dredge the swamp around the property to make it an "actual" 162-acre island. Thus the navigable canal around Elizabeth Park is actually a man-made canal, dug in 1921. The marina located at the park was opened in 1994.

#23 - THE THOROFARE
is a canal that runs completely through Grosse Ile. It begins just north of the Free Bridge on the Trenton Channel and runs through to the east side of Grosse Ile. In 1895, it was dredged and somewhat straightened from its original shallow marshy area. It is usually deep enough to be navigable to smaller boats, but its height is limited by low bridges.

#24 - WAYNE COUNTY FREE BRIDGE
(page 37) is generally called the "Free Bridge." It is built on what was the old Canada Southern Railroad Bridge, which came to Grosse Ile in 1873. It was a railroad bridge from 1873 to 1924. It was converted to an automobile bridge in 1931.

#25 - WATER'S EDGE COUNTRY CLUB.
It became the Island Boat and Country Club in 1956. The name was changed in 1973, when the club became municipally owned and operated.

#26 - HUMBUG ISLAND
(page 89) is an uninhabited island that had a hunting lodge located on it at the turn of the century. It is currently owned by Waste Management Corporation.

#27 - CALF ISLAND
(page 90) got its name from farmers keeping their young calves on the 11-acre island during the 1880s. A beautiful home was built on the island around 1914. Many influential businessmen and politicians used to frequent the island for hunting and other social occasions. The

home was furnished with magnificent carvings and antiques. The antiques began to disappear mysteriously in the 1950s when vandals began destroying the home. The home eventually burned to the ground in the early to mid-1960s. The foundation for the large home is still visible, hidden in all the underbrush. The island has been offered for sale in recent years.

#28 - SWAN ISLAND
(page 90) was originally known as "Snake Island." It was swampy unusable property before being drained and filled. The canal separating it from the mainland of Grosse Ile was dug in 1920s. The canal on the north end of the island that runs east into Frenchman Creek is know as Works Ditch. Swan Island was named for the Swan Family, who were early residents of Grosse Ile.

#29 - HUMBUG MARINA
(page 58) was started by Bill Heinrich in 1954. After a year or two of dredging, he turned the swamp area into room for about 100 boat wells. He sold Chris Craft boats there and eventually sold the operation to Evertte Hedke in 1964. Most of the canals throughout Gibraltar were dug in the 1920s, including the entrance to what is known as Humbug Marina. This main canal originally was dug off the Trenton Channel at about a 90-degree angle. This did not produce much water flow through the Gibraltar canal system. The city hired Mr. Heinrich to widen the opening of the canal as it comes off Trenton Channel to its current configuration. This was done in the mid-1950s and has resulted in a good current throughout the Gibraltar canals.

#30 - CELERON ISLAND
(page 90) is sometimes known as "Tawas" or "Taway." Its history goes back to the Potawatomi Indians. More recently it belonged to the Lowrie family from 1889, until they sold it in 1966. During that time, they built cottages, a boathouse, and a small farm, complete with barns. They sold the 125-acre island to the Celeron Island Corporation in 1966, who planned to develop it with 300 homes, a 200-boat marina, and a golf course. Some dredging actually started in 1967, but was stopped by a restraining order from the Grosse Ile Township. The buildings were burned down in the 1970s, and all that remains are old foundations being overgrown by underbrush.

#31 - FORD YACHT CLUB
was started in 1947 by a small group of Ford engineering employees. They leased 2.5 acres at their current location from Grosse Ile, and began their first building project in 1949. Dredging and docks were built beginning in 1950. By 1955, non-Ford employees were considered for membership. Construction of the large west boat basin began in 1960. They currently own approximately sixty acres, including Round Island, which is just east of their clubhouse, across from Frenchman's Creek. The club has room for approximately 275 boats.

#32 - FRENCHMAN'S CREEK
(page 72) runs from the Ford Yacht Club north and east back to Groh Road. It was originally dredged in the early 1920s. It was dredged again in 1990 to make it more navigable during low water.

#33 - GROSSE ILE AIRPORT

(Page 75) was built in 1927 on property previously owned by R. E. Olds, one of the early founders of the automobile. The grounds originally included the Olds mansion, located on Elba Island (Item # 39 on tour). It had a rich heritage as a United States Navy station for approximately forty years. It is also famous for being the home of the construction of the world's first all-metal dirigible, called the ZMC-2. A large checker-board hangar built for the dirigible construction was located on the airport grounds and became a landmark for local boaters until being torn down in 1960.

#34 - HICKORY ISLAND

is the southern most island of the Grosse Ile complex. It was a popular camping and picnic spot during the late 1800s. It became a summer colony consisting primarily of cottages prior to the popularity of automobiles. Private roads were built leading to the island, and many of the cottages were converted to year-round residences.

#35 - HICKORY ISLAND

is another one of the smaller islands contained in Grosse Ile Township. It is the home of the Grosse Ile Yacht Club (GIYC), which was formed in 1934. Their first clubhouse was a converted boathouse dragged onto shore on "Peek-a-boo" Island. The current building was started in 1949. More recent additions were completed in 1994. The open stair steps leading to their inside upper level were made from large timbers removed from the Trenton Channel in front of Liggett's Boat Works. The timbers were removed from the water and laid on the ground along Riverside Drive for several years drying out. A resourceful Grosse Ile Yacht Club member eventually obtained the old pilings and had them sawed into useful steps for their clubhouse.

Fig. 77

#36 - SUGAR ISLAND

(page 91) has a long heritage dating back to 1817. It became a major amusement park in the late 1800s. Attractions included a roller coaster, dancing pavilion, restaurants, beaches, covered waiting room at the ferry dock, bicycle track, baseball diamonds, rowboat rental liveries, etc. Most people traveled to the island on large ferryboats. The *Tashmoo* was one of the more popular. This boat left the large cement docks off Sugar Island (portions of these docks still remain) with 1,400 passengers and an orchestra aboard in 1936, headed toward

Detroit. While going through the Hole-in-the-Wall, it apparently hit a rock and tore a hole in its bottom. The captain got the boat to the Canadian shore, where the passengers were unloaded, mostly unaware of the eminent danger. Once unloaded, the boat sank to the bottom in the shallow waters next to Amherstburg. This was the beginning of the decline for tourists coming to Sugar Island. Little was done to the island during the late 1930s and 40s. The buildings and amusement rides fell into disrepair and were vandalized. The large dance pavilion burned down in 1954. After several failed attempts to develop the 35-acre island into homesites and a marina, it was sold to a private individual in 1985. It is still privately owned, although many local boaters make use of the sand beach. Many of the original park and building foundations are still visible among underbrush on the interior of the island.

#37 - ELBA-MAR BOAT CLUB (EMBC)

The Elba-Mar Boat Club was formed in 1953. The name was derived from "Elba," being close to Elba Island, and "Mar," short for "marsh," because it was a marshy area. The first boat docks were built by the membership in 1954, followed by construction of a clubhouse in 1955. The original club was purchased by forty-four members in 1962, forming the Grosse Ile Development Corporation. This property was then sold to the Elba-Mar Boat Club in 1974. The clubhouse was remodeled three times between 1970 and 1980. It currently has approximately 300 active members and room to moor 180 boats.

#38 - THE OLDS MANSION

was built in 1916 by the founder of one of the oldest car companies in the United States, R. E. Olds. It is located on Elba Island, which is another of the smaller islands that are part of Grosse Ile Township. It remained in the Olds family until around 1930. Major features of the mansion included a built-in pipe organ, game room, and a large ballroom making up most of the third (top) floor. The Olds family spent sum-

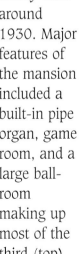

Figure 78

This picture of Sugar Island was taken from the Olds Mansion on Elba Island, circa 1920. Note the roller coaster ride in the center of the picture.
(Courtesy of the Grosse Ile Historical Society)

Fig. 78

mers in the house, along with five servants and a crew of five who maintained the yachts. One of the yachts was a 100+ footer. R. E. Olds was known as a very friendly person, who always spoke to the servants and often passed out gifts at holidays. Visitors included George Eastman (founder of Eastman Kodak), Harvey Firestone (tires), and Henry Ford. Originally there was a boathouse, ice house, and horse barn on the property. The mansion was included in the parcel of land that the Grosse Ile airport was built on in 1927, and was used as a clubhouse when the airport was first opened. It served as a U.S.O. center in World War II and was later sold for back taxes. The mansion was more recently converted into seven apartments.

ed on the island. It was common during the mid-1970s for the family to have seventy to eighty people on the island for weekend social gatherings. Vandals and fire eventually destroyed the building.

#40 - POWDER HOUSE ISLAND
is sometimes called Dynamite Island. Recent local folklore claims it got its name by being the storage area for the explosives needed during the construction of the Livingstone Channel. There are stories about local duck hunters firing into the island during that time, setting off an explosion heard all over the Downriver area. However, looking at nautical charts of the area from around 1903, before the Livingstone Channel was started, shows the island was there and already named Powder House Island. It is probable that the island was used as a storage area during one of the early dredging operations prior to the Livingstone Channel project.

#41 - STONY ISLAND
(page 109) was the headquarters for the construction workers who built the Livingstone Channel from 1907 through 1912. There were over thirty homes on the island, along with a general store and a large hall that served as a school, church, and dance hall. Prior to that, the Canada Southern Railroad had a railroad bridge between Trenton and Grosse Ile (the current County Free Bridge structure) and another between Grosse Ile and Stony Island. There was a dock on Stony Island where a large railroad ferry transported rail cars back and forth to Canada.

Figure 79

The Olds Mansion built by the automobile pioneer for a summer residence in 1916. It had many famous visitors over the years. It became part of the Grosse Ile Airport property in the 1920s, when it housed the U.S.O. It is currently an apartment house.

Fig. 79

#39 - FOX ISLAND
(page 109) is a private island now owned by the Bob Brown family. It was previously owned by the Dominic Gorno family, who had a summer cottage locat-

This allowed a direct rail route from the midwest United States to and from Buffalo, N.Y. This rail service lasted from 1873 to 1888, when it no longer was profitable. Stony Island is currently for sale, and there are rumors around that local investors are trying to buy it to develop it with expensive homes. This includes rebuilding the old railroad bridge with a modern automobile bridge. Time will tell!

#42 - PREVIOUS LOCATION OF RAILROAD BRIDGE TO STONY ISLAND

(page 109). In 1873, a railroad bridge connecting Grosse Ile and Stony Island was built. The rail service lasted until 1888. The bridge fell into disrepair following that and was removed in 1913. The stone abutment at the east end of Grosse Ile Parkway that supported one end of the bridge is still evident, as is the peninsula that was built on the west end of Stony Island as the bridge approach. The original cement pilings that supported the bridge are still submerged under water, so care (with local knowledge) must be used while boating in this area. Just west of the old bridge abutment on Grosse Ile is the location of the railroad depot. This building is now the home of The Grosse Ile Historical Society.

#43 - THE REMAINS OF A SUNKEN SHIP

can be seen along the west Livingstone Channel cofferdam approximately one quarter of a mile south of the Hole-in-the-Wall. The steel ribs of the approximately 100-foot ship are still visible above the water. There were several ships about this size used as sleeping barracks for the workers during the construction of the Livingstone Channel in the 1907 to 1912 period. Local mariners speculate that this old ship was one of those barracks, which either sank or was scuttled after the project was completed. .

#44 - HOLE-IN-THE-WALL

is a popular landmark used by local

Fig. 80

boaters when describing their location when boating in this area. As with all of the small finger-type islands, or cofferdams, bordering the Livingstone Channel, they were formed during the construction of the channel. The stone cofferdams north of the Hole-in-the-Wall were primarily built during the construction of the original phase of the Livingstone Channel during 1907 to 1912. That whole area was dammed off, the water was drained, and the channel was dug as dry land. The stone dams south of the Hole-in-the-Wall are the result of additional dredging of the channel in the mid-1950s.

Figure 80

Steel ribs sticking out of the water from the remains of a partially sunken ship. It was probably used during construction of the Livingstone Channel during 1907 to 1912

#45 - BOBLO ISLAND MARINA
was a popular spot for local, as well as long-distance, boaters to stop for day trips to the amusement park, or for overnight stays. Prior to the amusement park closing in the fall of 1993, reservations were required on weekends to ensure a spot, as it was normally full. As with all Canadian ports, it was necessary for non-Canadian boaters to register with the Canadian authorities when staying at the marina.

#46- BOBLO OBSERVATION TOWER
is 340 feet tall and was built around 1984 when AAA owned the amusement park. It is the highest man-made structure in the county. The observation deck rotates. On a clear day it was possible to see some of the islands of Lake Erie. It is one of the few rides in the amusement park that was not, and will not be, sold off since the park closed in 1993. It is planned to leave this tower as a Boblo Island landmark.

#47 - REMAINS OF BOBLO BLOCKHOUSE
(page 98) are still seen on the south end of what was known as Bois Blanc Island. There were three of the blockhouses built by the British in 1839, when their headquarters were located in Amherstburg. Private owners bought Bois Blanc Island in 1869 and built a lavish estate for entertaining and hunting. They used at least one of the blockhouses for their headquarters during that time.

#48 - BOBLO ISLAND LIGHTHOUSE
(page 99) was built on what was then the south end of Bois Blanc Island in 1836. It was manually operated until the late 1920s. The top structure was van-dalized and burned down in 1954. In 1961, it was declared to be of Canadian historic significance, and Fort Malden was given responsibility for its care.

#49 - WHITE SANDS AREA
is part of the cofferdam system produced when the Livingstone and Amherstburg channels were deepened and widened in the mid-1950s. Boblo Island's natural shape ended just south of the old lighthouse prior to the dredging projects. The White Sands Beach became a very popular picnic and camping spot for area boaters until the current owner of Boblo Island, John Oram, bought the island. The Canadian government actually owns the White Sands area, and leased it to the new Boblo owner. In the fall of 1994, he posted "NO TRESPASSING" signs and used heavy equipment to destroy the beach so it could no longer be used as a picnic or camping area. This continues to raise controversy among local boaters and their families.

#50 - AMHERSTBURG - BOBLO FERRY DOCK
provided the shortest ferryboat ride to the Boblo Island amusement park. It was the Canadian home for the small Boblo ferryboats. After the big Boblo ferry boats discontinued running out of Detroit in 1991, many U.S. citizens drove across the bridge or tunnel to Windsor, down to Amherstburg, and took the short ferry ride to Boblo. One of the small Boblo ferryboats (Friendship) is currently moored at the Portofino Restaurant on the Trenton Channel in Wyandotte, where it is used for dinner and dance cruises.

#51 - BOBLO FERRY DOCK
is where the large and small ferryboats dropped off and picked up their passen-

gers visiting the amusement park. It was formed by sinking a large barge. The amusement park at Boblo Island operated from 1898 until 1993. In its heyday, up to the 1980s, nearly one million people annually visited the park and enjoyed the thirty-two rides and picnic areas. The current Boblo owner is selling lots for homes and other developments on the island.

#52 - CAR FERRY DOCK FOR BOBLO

facilitates two car ferries that transfer cars and trucks back and forth from the mainland to Boblo Island. One ferry can carry six cars, the other twelve. They can make the trip across the river every five minutes. Only Boblo property owners' cars are allowed on the island.

#53 - DUFFY'S TAVERN

(page 83) began as the Deerhead Club on Sandwich Street following World War I. It was established by Alexander Duff, son of early Amherstburg residents, when he returned from the war. He later moved the restaurant business downtown to a building known as Bulluck's Tavern. He moved again into the Fraser Building, where he added a tavern and changed the name to Duffy's Tavern. The business was eventually sold to Zarko Vucini and Mike Jojich. In 1964, the building was completely renovated by its present owner, Zarko Vucini. Duffy's Tavern now has seating for 400 people, and docking for seventy boats. It is a popular stop for local boaters from both sides of the river, as well as a stopover for transient boaters traveling through the area.

#54 - KING'S NAVY PARK

(page 76) is the location where many British ships were built prior to the War of 1812. The area contained storehouses, timber yard, sawmill, and other facilities necessary to build ships, including large docks. All sorts of ships were built there, ranging from small boats to full-sized three-masted battleships. The British ships who battled Commander Perry in the famous naval battle near Put-In-Bay sailed from this port. All facilities were intentionally burned following the British defeat in 1813, to keep the Americans from using them. British shipbuilding was moved to the Georgian Bay area, further away from American threats. Plans began in 1977 to make the area into a park, which opened in 1980.

#55 - FORT MALDEN

(page 76) was built to replace the British fort in Detroit, which was turned over to the newly formed United States in 1796 as a result of the Treaty of Paris in 1783. Some of the materials required to build the fort were actually floated down the river from Detroit. Forces stationed at Fort Malden captured an American ship traveling up the river during early stages of the War of 1812. Troops from this location were involved in many battles with U.S. troops, the most famous being with Commander Perry near Put-In-Bay. The fort was intentionally destroyed following the war and taken over by the United States, who partially rebuilt it. It was turned back over to the British in 1815, and it deteriorated and was rebuilt several times as military conditions dictated. It was used as an insane asylum from 1859 to 1870. The property was auctioned off in 1875, and parts of the buildings were used as a wood mill until around 1918. The property became primarily used for residential use until around 1940, when it became a locally operated museum. It has been run by the Canadian Federal Government since the mid-1950s as a historic site and museum.

#56 - HORSESHOE ANCHORAGE,

at the north end of Boblo Island, is the result of dredging in the Amherstburg and Livingstone channels in the mid-1950s. The stone dikes were produced by stacking up the material dug out while deepening and widening the channels. In the shallow bay between the "Horseshoe" and the north end of Boblo, there are remains of three old wooden barges used during the dredging projects. The wooden frameworks are located in shallow water along the south edge of the Horseshoe and still very visible. The entire bay where they are located is quite shallow, so extreme care must be taken if exploring there with a power boat. This horseshoe-shaped area at the north end of Boblo Island was a U-shaped island, forming the protected anchorage area until the fall of 1996. Prior to that time, a careful boater could pass between Horseshoe and Boblo Island. However, in the fall of 1996, a stone dike was built connecting the Horseshoe with Boblo, making it impossible to pass between the two islands.

#57 - CRYSTAL BAY

is the weekend home for many local boaters. It is one of the most popular anchorage spots in the Great Lakes. As with all of the stone dikes and cofferdams in the lower Detroit River, Crystal Bay was formed by the material removed while dredging to deepen and widen the Amherstburg and Livingstone channels. The extreme northwest wall of Crystal Bay was produced during the original

Livingstone Channel project of 1907-1912. The remaining walls were produced during dredging projects in the mid-1950s. Many boaters claim Crystal Bay as their home port, as does the informal "Crystal Bay Yacht Club." On most summer weekends, among the hundreds of boats, several barbecue boats cruise around selling sandwiches, pop, and other essentials. All but the extreme northwest part of the bay is in Canadian waters, so Canadian laws apply and are enforced for Crystal Bay visitors.

There is an enclosed area along the north east end of Crystal Bay known as Hidden Lake. This was originally an enclosed lake when the cofferdams were built, forming Crystal Bay. The lake was fed by underground streams passing through the limestone, making it an extremely clean lake popular with the few swimmers and scuba divers who knew about it. Its popularity led people to remove loose stones from the dike that separates it from Crystal Bay, making it accessible by boat from Crystal Bay.

There is another enclosed area on the northeast side of Crystal Bay, known as Little Crystal. This is also accessible by a careful boater from its south end. Up until the late 1980s, there was a large tree with a rope tied to its top located at the very north end of Little Crystal. It was used for years for climbing up onto the bank and swinging down into the water. Many locals still have scars from scraping the gravel bank on their swing down if they did not grab the rope at the right height. Apparently some father became angry when his son or daughter came home all scraped up from an ill-fated jump from the infamous rope and came back with a chain saw and cut the tree down.

#58 - DUFF'S RESTAURANT

is the home of the Crystal Bay barbecue boats. These boats cruise Crystal Bay on summer weekends and holidays selling sandwiches cooked onboard, soft drinks, and other munchies. Duff's also has a restaurant that features summer weekend breakfast buffets, fishing supplies, gas, and docking facilities for seasonal boaters.

#59 - GROSSE ILE LIGHTHOUSE

was originally built in 1894. It was rebuilt into its present structure in 1906. The original lighthouse keepers had to maintain the kerosene lamps, clean the lenses, paint the buildings, and do whatever else was necessary to maintain the grounds. The light was electrified about 1929 and was in operation until 1948. In 1965, the Grosse Ile Township purchased the light from the U.S. Department of Interior with funds provided by the Grosse Ile Historical Society. Occasionally the society has an open house where tours are conducted in the old lighthouse. It went through a considerable facelift beginning in 1996, when the original siding was replaced with cypress wood originally used in pickle vats.

There is a sister lighthouse built from the same plans, currently located at the Buffalo Launch Club on Grand Island, just across the Niagara River from Buffalo, N.Y. It is the same size and shape as the Grosse Ile Light.

#60 - THE THOROFARE

begins just north of the Grosse Ile Lighthouse. It cuts across Grosse Ile to just north of the Wayne County Free Bridge. See #22 for more details.

#61 - THE FISHER MANSION

was built by Charles T. Fisher, one of the famous Fisher brothers who formed Fisher Body, Division of General Motors. It was built as a summer home and was one of the last summer mansions of this type built on Grosse Ile.

#62 - PREVIOUS LOCATION OF MAMAJUDA ISLAND

(page 110). There was originally a 20- to 30-acre island located between the north end of Grosse Ile and Fighting Island called Mamajuda. It was an important landmark for mariners during the early shipping industry. So important, in fact, that a lighthouse was constructed on it in 1849. The lighthouse keeper had a home and small farm on the island where he raised a family. High water in the 1950s took its toll on the buildings and lighthouse foundation and eventually washed the

Figure 81

The Grosse Ile Light was originally built in 1894 and rebuilt into its current form in 1906. It is currently owned and maintained by the Grosse Ile Historical Society.

Fig. 81

Figure 82

The Fisher Mansion built as a summer home by Charles Fisher, one of the famous Fisher brothers.

whole visible island away. By the early 1960s, only a few large boulders, tree stumps, and sandy shoal were all that was left. During the early 1940s, the U.S. government proposed connecting Mamajuda Island with Mud and Grassy islands to form a large 680-acre island. Local protest derailed this plan before it

Fig. 82

ever materialized.

#63 - HENNEPIN POINT

is primarily a man-made island at the north end of Grosse Ile. It was originally a shallow marshy area. It became a dumping area for the chemical companies in Wyandotte during the 1890s. There has been no dumping since the mid-1980s. Major sink holes developed in the center of the area in 1971, when underground salt mines caved in. The mines were some 1,400 feet below the surface. The whole area is fenced off, posted "NO TRESPASSING," and patrolled by security personnel.

This ends the **GUIDED HISTORICAL BOAT TOUR ON THE RIVER**. Hope you enjoyed it and had a safe trip.

EPILOG

This book is the result of several years of document research, including interviewing local residents about Downriver history and folklore. Once this research process began, it never ended. Current events soon became history, and people kept coming out of the woodwork with interesting stories of the glorious days gone by. I finally had to draw a line in the sand and publish the information I had, even as new and interesting lore became available. It certainly is not in my immediate plans to write a sequel to *Our "Downriver" River*, but I can visualize there is enough interesting information still out there that would be of interest to many. With this in mind, I solicit any additional nautical historical data about the Downriver area that any readers may want to contribute toward any future project. Pictures and personal (family/friend's) stories about past experiences, such as rumrunning and activities on the smaller islands, are examples of topics that many find intriguing. If I do not have the time and/or energy to put any additional information into a meaningful format, I would certainly make sure it gets into appropriate archives of the local historical societies. At the same time, if any readers have found any gross errors in this book's text, feel free to contact the author. I can be reached at 810-947-1615.

Additional copies of this book can be obtained by calling the author and are available in most downriver yacht clubs and historical societies as well as several local businesses.

THE DETROIT RIVER LIGHT

by Sue and Leo Kuschel

The Detroit River Light is located four miles south of Boblo Island marking the mouth of the Detroit River. In 1873 the Lighthouse Board wanted to construct a light at Bar Point Shoal. Many ships had run aground there, where they have to make a turn to head into the Detroit River. The Canadian government established a lightship on the shoal in 1875. The problem continued because the lightship light was not very powerful, and there were many different lights in the area from the shoreline and from passing ships that caused the navigators to became confused. The United States Congress finally approved $60,000 for building of the Detroit River Light in 1882. Another $18,000 was needed before the project was completed in 1885.

Captain C. E. L. B. Davis of the U.S. Army Corps of Engineers designed and supervised the entire building project. Test borings were made in 1882 and construction began in 1884. A timber crib 45 feet wide, 90 feet long, and 18 feet high was built at Amherstburg and towed to the site and sunk in 22 feet of water on July 3, 1884. It took about two months to fill it with concrete. Construction began on the pier using cut stone blocks. The overall pier dimensions were 43 feet wide, 90 feet long, 15 feet high, and it extended four feet below the water line. The block laying was complete on November 21, 1884, but settling of the crib and pier was uneven, causing the whole foundation to be unlevel. This required 550 tons of rubble stone to be loaded onto the high side of the pier.

When work resumed in the spring, the pier was level, allowing construction of the light tower and fog signal building.

The light was first lit on August 20, 1885. The walls of the conical tower are made of brick and are 12 inches thick. The 10-sided outer surface of the lantern is cast iron plate, surrounded by a round watch room. It is 49 feet high.

The lower portion of the tower is painted white with the upper portion being black, which creates a distinctive day-mark pattern for ships heading north into the river. The tower is situated on the pier so that it faces south, with the fog signal building behind the tower. The fog signal building is also painted white with a red roof. At the turn of the century, this building was painted brown, which was common practice with the lighthouse service at that time.

Through the years the light source in this station has changed several times. It was usually a classical Fresnel lens with a bullseye, meaning there were four to six sides with a round center. The distance the light could be seen over the water has varied from 14 to 22 miles.

In 1930, the Lighthouse Board established two-way radio communication on the Stannard Rock Light in Lake Superior and on the Detroit River Light. This work began with construction of radio beacon transmitters that were salvaged from other projects, which resulted in considerable savings over buying new equipment. The equipment has been improved considerably through the years. Heavy ship traffic over the years kept the Detroit light keepers busy saving lives and property. These endeavors were helped by radio communication to

Figure 83

Copy of Leo Kuschel's print of the Detroit Lighthouse. (Courtesy of Leo Kuschel)

land stations. The pier has been struck numerous times by lake freighters and small boats during its long service.

We have been out to the light many times. Three were most memorable. The first time was with the U.S. Coast Guard

on their 32-footer. A few years later we were able to fly over the light in a Canadian Coast Guard helicopter. Most recently, in 1993, we organized and supervised a tour of the off-shore lights in the western end of Lake Erie. This was a two-day cruise sponsored by the Great Lakes Lighthouse Keepers Association, with an overnight stay in Port Clinton, Ohio.

This last visit was on the cruise boat the Diamond Belle, with her owner Bill Hoey from Grosse Ile at the helm as Captain. A pleasant addition to the expedition was having a dive team from the Dossin Great Lakes Museum in Detroit on board. Captain Hoey brought the boat up to the Detroit Light and we had live, on deck, television coverage of the divers exploring the submerged crib below the light. They even brought up some china cups with the infamous zebra mussels attached to them. One of the members of this dive team was our friend and local celebrity Mal Sillars. This was all to the delight of the 250 lighthouse enthusiasts who had joined us for this Lake Erie cruise. Now the light has been automated, with the power source being solar light panels. The radio beacon and fog signal are also automated. Because Lake Erie is so shallow, storms and subsequent rough water can come up very quickly. When this happens, the sight of the Detroit River Light coming into view is a most welcome relief for returning local boaters, because they know they are almost home!

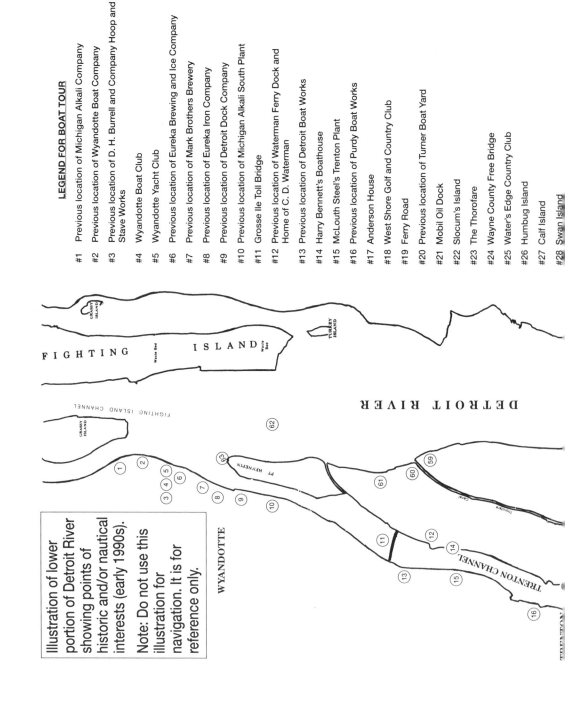

Illustration of lower portion of Detroit River showing points of historic and/or nautical interests (early 1990s).

Note: Do not use this illustration for navigation. It is for reference only.

LEGEND FOR BOAT TOUR

#1 Previous location of Michigan Alkali Company
#2 Previous location of Wyandotte Boat Company
#3 Previous location of D. H. Burrell and Company Hoop and Stave Works
#4 Wyandotte Boat Club
#5 Wyandotte Yacht Club
#6 Previous location of Eureka Brewing and Ice Company
#7 Previous location of Mark Brothers Brewery
#8 Previous location of Eureka Iron Company
#9 Previous location of Detroit Dock Company
#10 Previous location of Michigan Alkali South Plant
#11 Grosse Ile Toll Bridge
#12 Previous location of Waterman Ferry Dock and Home of C. D. Waterman
#13 Previous location of Detroit Boat Works
#14 Harry Bennett's Boathouse
#15 McLouth Steel's Trenton Plant
#16 Previous location of Purdy Boat Works
#17 Anderson House
#18 West Shore Golf and Country Club
#19 Ferry Road
#20 Previous location of Turner Boat Yard
#21 Mobil Oil Dock
#22 Slocum's Island
#23 The Thorofare
#24 Wayne County Free Bridge
#25 Water's Edge Country Club
#26 Humbug Island
#27 Calf Island
#28 Swan Island